Loving to Audition

Smith and Kraus, Inc.
Career Development Series

Technique Books

The Actor's Chekhov by Jean Hackett

Anne Bogart: Viewpoints ed. by Michael B. Dixon and Joel A. Smith

Auditioning for the Musical Theatre by Donald Oliver

The Camera Smart Actor by Richard Brestoff

The Great Acting Teachers and their Methods by Richard Brestoff

The Sanford Meisner Approach Workbook I: An Actor's Workbook
by Larry Silverberg

The Sanford Meisner Approach Workbook II: Emotional Freedom
by Larry Silverberg

A Shakespearean Actor Prepares by Adrian Brine and Michael York

Actor's Guides

The Actor's Guide to Qualified Acting Coaches: Los Angeles
by Larry Silverberg

The Actor's Guide to Qualified Acting Coaches: New York
by Larry Silverberg

Hot Tips for Cold Readings: Some Do's and Don'ts for Actors at Auditions
by Nina Finburgh

The Job Book I: 100 Acting Jobs for Actors by Glenn Alterman

The Job Book II: 100 Day Jobs for Actors by Glenn Alterman

The Smith and Kraus Monologue Index ed. by Karen Morris

*What to Give Your Agent for Christmas and 100 Other Tips for the
Working Actor* by Glenn Alterman

Loving to Audition

the audition workbook for actors

by Larry Silverberg

Career Development Series

SK
A Smith and Kraus Book

A Smith and Kraus Book
Published by Smith and Kraus, Inc.
PO Box 127, Lyme, NH 03768

Cover and Text Design by Julia Hill
Cover Art by Irene Kelly

First Edition: February 1997
10 9 8 7 6 5 4 3 2 1

The Library of Congress Cataloging-In-Publication Data
Silverberg, Larry, 1959–
Loving to audition: the audition workbook for actors / by Larry Silverberg. --1st ed.
p.   cm.   -- (Career development series)
ISBN 1-57525-007-1
1. Acting—Auditions. I. Title. II. Series.
PN2071.A92S56   1996
792'.028—dc21   96-40242
                         CIP

Contents

Section One
Bringing a Monologue to Life: Monologue Technique

Section Two
Loving to Audition: A Living Approach

Listen!

After you finish this book,
you will never audition for another part.

(I'll say that in another way.)

After you read this book,
you will continue to go to auditions,
but when you get there,
you will not audition for anything.

In fact, from this point on,
YOUR AUDITIONING DAYS ARE OVER!

Does this sound absurd?
Unimaginable?
Isn't this a book on auditioning?

Let me explain...

Obviously, I was trying to grab your attention. But I do want you to give some real consideration to the concept that an audition is an event, a happening, not an activity. **It is something you go to, not something you do.**

The whole idea of "auditioning" is one that undermines the actors sense of power and his or her true talents. The way we hold the concept of "auditioning," can debilitate and cripple us.

Let me ask you a question. If you were to enroll in a four-year acting training program, would you hope to come out of the school:

1. Having become an adept, agile, versatile, skilled and courageous artist of the theatre.

– or –

2. Having become a knees shaking pleaser, pleader and beseecher, a hireling who tiptoes from audition to audition attempting to make your most humble and earnest petition to be given a job?

If you are more aligned with number one, why don't you and I abolish the idea of "auditioning" altogether. Let's shift our focus from going into the audition and hoping to be "wanted," to going into the audition and giving a great performance!

Don't you think that what every director and producer really want to see you do is some great acting? **Isn't that what you really want to do?**

Are you with me on this?

You are?

Then Welcome!

Yes, this book is all about helping you become powerfully effective in your audition performances. And though our focus here is on the audition event, this book is even more so about re-igniting your passion to act, making direct contact with your deep need to express yourself and an unleashing of your unique spirit. Now, don't you think those are some important things to bring along with you to every audition?

I believe you will discover in new ways, as you "do" this book, that your own vision of your work as an actor and of the difference you hope to make, is important and necessary. That YOU are important and necessary. That YOU have a contribution to make. That, in our world of mostly imitation bacon, especially in the world of acting, we need the REAL YOU more than ever!

When we stop and really take a look, it's so clear that life is a most surprising and miraculous adventure. Should our searching to be a fantastically alive and authentic actor be anything less? I have tried to create a book that reflects that ongoing journey; an acting workbook that offers you a process of taking a deeper look inside of yourself, as you become vitally connected to everyone and everything in the world around you. I think that you are going to find that the realm of performing at auditions has greater potential for personal creativity than you might have imagined, and that it can even be fun! Wouldn't that be great?

In Section One of the book, I will be teaching you a very specific and exciting approach to working on audition material; techniques that will give you a most personal way to bring the monologue to life. In Section Two, we will explore from many angles, our attitudes toward auditions and how we can actually turn auditions into occasions filled with true satisfaction and joy.

So, are you ready?

Then turn the page...

Section One

Bringing a Monologue to Life: Monologue Technique

chapter 1

Building the Basis
from Which to Act the Part

You know, there are a lot of books which offer all kinds of audition tactics and strategies. Personally, I'm not into tactics. And I've never been interested in quick tips. There's no easy formula to unleash your "talent." There certainly is no "one right way"—not when it comes to working on the part and not when it comes to preparing for the audition.

I do believe though that there is one major requirement in finding the best audition material and that is that **YOU absolutely love it**. And by love it, I mean that it hits you where you live, that when you read the monologue it does something to you—it makes you want to stand up and thank God for the gift of life, or it leaves you frozen in your seat unable to utter a sound, or you read it and weep uncontrollably, or it makes you so angry that you rip the damn thing up, or it keeps you awake all night because you just can't shake it. Listen, if the piece doesn't connect with you on a deep level, why the hell bother with it? Of course, I've seen situations where a college acting program will send you a few monologues to choose from for your audition. If you're lucky, one will reach out and grab you. But normally, you are the one who finds your own monologues, so why not choose the most personally appetizing material you can bite into? And when your own excitement is the key prerequisite, you're no longer just "doing it for them." You are doing it for you first—because it is meaningful to you, it is important to you, there is something in it that you want to express, to share, and the thought of getting inside those words lights your fire!

Now, your primary concern need not be whether the monologues you choose are used often as audition pieces, your primary concern must always be in bringing a vivid and passionate life to the material you work on. At the same time, it sure doesn't hurt to do monologues that few casting people are aware of. Directors and producers will tell you that they just love to see pieces they have never seen before and that it improves your chances that, after the fifty other auditions they've already seen, they are going to really pay attention to you. And, in addition to plays, there are many other sources of great monologues: novels and short stories, available screenplays, in movies and on TV (keep a little tape recorder handy), in newspapers and magazines, and in some well-done monologue collections for actors. (And here's a plug for my publishers, Smith & Kraus. Call their 800 number and request one of their catalogues. They have a whole series of monologue books, as well as acting technique books and collections of plays.) Obviously, part of your job is to be on constant lookout for material that turns you on—whether you use it for an audition or not.

Let's move forward now and explore some of the dramatic elements found in good audition material. To do that, I'm going to share with you two speeches from a great play by one of my favorite playwrights. The play is *Savage In Limbo* by John Patrick Shanley.

Now, wait a minute...Before you read the monologues, make sure you are not limited in time right now. If you are, come back to this when you are not rushed.

If you are going to continue right now, I want you to get your-self in a quiet, comfortable place. Get rid of any distractions so that you can relax and give the material your full attention. Obviously, I am suggesting that the way in which you read is significant. I say that your first encounter with the words is an important time to simply "be with" the script, allowing the script to "work on you" without doing anything about it. Many actors get off to a bad start with the script because they are half reading and half "blocking the performance" in their heads. As best you can, try not to be concerned with anything related to peforming when you are first reading the script. You must be listening; if you are simply and quietly listening, the words will speak to you—and you need to be there to receive them. So in that manner, I want you to read the monologues. First read Tony's speech. Read it THREE times and then turn to the writ-ing exercise on the following page. When you finish writing, contin-ue on to Savage's speech and do the same—read it three times and turn to the writing exercise.

1. Tony Aronica

"I was in my car outside this place over the weekend. I hadda a couple a drinks and I was a little fuzzy, so I was waitin till I cleared. It was dark. I was sittin there. And this unknown girl got in. She just got in the car. And she started talkin to me. She started rappin to me about the Soviet Union. Yeah. 'Bout their economy. Housin. How they feel about China bein right there. Everything. Everything about the Soviet Union. She musta talked for two hours. Russian paranoia. Tass. The Gulag. I'm sittin there an I'm takin this in. The Trans-Siberian Railroad. What kinda tanks they got in Eastern Europe. Why they need

American wheat. And then she was finished. She'd told me everything she knew. So I took her in the back seat and I banged her. And do you know something? It was the best. It was the best I ever had. And it whadn't cause she knew a lotta tricks or like that. It was cause she'd told me about the Soviet Union. And then she left. Now here's the thing. She was very ugly. I don't even wanna talk about how she looked. Mucho ugly. I didn't think I could ever be with a woman like that. But it came about outta whatever, happenstance, and I was. And it turned out to be better than what I went after. Do you see what I mean? Do you see what I'm comin towards? I always went for the girl like you. And what finally fuckin come to me, what finally fuckin penetrated the wall here, was there was somethin else. Somethin I never even thought about, didn't have a clue about. When I talked to you, I called it ugly girls. I don't know what to call it. There's other people. Like in science fiction. Another dimension right there but you can't see it. I got into it for a minute by accident. Through a crack. I caught a flash. The dimension a ugly girls. I'm like one a those guys inna factory and they bring in all new machines. That's what I feel like. Like I gotta retrain or I'm gonna lose my place. Some girls you look at some girls you don't. I wanna see the things I didn't see before an let the stuff I was lookin at go by. I've done the fuckin thing we're in, Linda. I've been with you, I talked to you. I know what that is. That's what I meant when I said you didn't know nothin, but I whadn't sayin it right. You look at what I look at. You know what I know. I wanna look at somethin else. I wanna know somethin else. I'm thirty-two years old. I wanna change."

Please write about the thoughts, feelings, impressions and images Tony's speech sparked in you.

_____

_____

_____

_____

_____

_____

_____

_____

_____

_____

_____

_____

_____

_____

_____

_____

_____

_____

_____

_____

_____

_____

2. Denise Savage

"I don't care. I don't care how you think about me. What d'you want? You want me to act like somebody on TV? This one got this one way an that's how they are? I don't know how I am, who I am. I don't know what I believe. I don't know where to go to find out. I don't know what to do to be the one person that somewhere inside I wanna be. I don't know nothin but the one thing: I gotta move. And you, too. This whole world I'm in's gotta break up an move. We're on the cliff. We were born here. Well, do you wanna die on the cliff? Do you wanna die in bed? Do you think you're gonna live forever? They told us if you jump off the cliff, you die. And you probably do, but fuck it. Fuck it. We don't know that. You don't know nothin you ain't done, an nobody can tell you nothin. Ain't you tired a livin if this is all livin is? And you know it's not. I may be an asshole and I may not know what to do, but you hear what I'm sayin to you, dammit you do. In your heart you do. This is not life. This is not life. This is not life. Ugly women, right Tony? Somethin else. I don't care what. God, gimme somethin else cause this is definitely not it. New eyes new ears new hands. Gimme back my soul from where you took it, gimme back my friends, gimme back my priests an my father, and take this goddamn virginity from off my life. HUNGER HUNGER HUNGER. If somebody don't gimme somethin, I'm gonna die. I wanna play pool. Somebody play pool with me. I come in here a lotta nights, a lotta nights, an I play pool by myself. I like the game. You hit the white ball, and that ball hits another, and it goes somewhere. When I first started, I didn't mind playin alone. But you get tired of it. The balls don't do nothin unless you make 'em do it. It's all you. They're just like stones. It's like I'm some woman lives inna cave and plays with stones. Somebody play pool with me. You be the cue ball. Hit me and I'll fly. You don't wanna jump yourself, push me off. You can't keep up your courage alone, playin with stones."

Please write about the thoughts, feelings, impressions and images Savage's speech sparked in you.

Go back and take another look at the two speeches and find any dramatic similarities. I'm not talking about structure or anything so technical. We have caught these two characters in a particular moment of time and they are expressing something to someone else. In a broad sense, what kinds of things are alike in the two pieces? Use this page to write about that.

_____

_____

_____

_____

_____

_____

_____

_____

_____

_____

_____

_____

_____

_____

_____

_____

_____

_____

_____

_____

In the latter chapters of this book, we will be discussing the fundamental skills of great acting: **really listening, really doing and fully doing what you are doing, living in-the-moment, expressing oneself authentically, being in response to your partners on stage, embracing what's happening and being open and available.** We will be talking about the urgency of **building a foundation** for becoming an artist as an actor. (When you want to build a home of lasting value, you make sure the foundation is very strong!) Now, although this is where many actors stop—as do many teachers of acting, it's only the beginning of the story. The actor must become equally adroit as an investigator of the script, learning how to ask the important **questions of interpretation**. And, in fact, interpretation is always much more about asking great questions than finding great answers. It is the questions that excite our "actors imaginations" and it is our imagination that propels us into taking action.

To begin, we have to know how to look at a script as an actor. So, let's take a look at three very basic things we will find in all well written scripts.

1. WANT!

Every character, in every play is trying to accomplish something. And what the character wants to accomplish, get or have happen, is always personally meaningful to them. Have you heard the term "spine" used in relation to acting? It's a wonderful metaphor for how we must begin to grapple with finding our way into the script and into the character. Think for a moment about our own spines. The spine is a bony column, but not a solid one, it is made up of many segments—the vertebrae—which are linked by flexible joints. Not only does the spine form our body's main structural support, it offers a tunnellike space that houses the spinal cord. The spinal cord carries sensory impulses from the trunk and limbs to the brain and it returns commands from the brain to the muscles. **So everything we do in life and a lot of how we perceive our lives is somehow influenced by the condition of our spine—and our spine is in constant adjustment to the conditions of our life.**

As actors, we must bring ourselves into a personal relationship with **the character's "spine."** Without this, we have absolutely no basis from which to act the part. This means that we must first have a way of exploring the script as we mine for this thing called "spine" and then we must have ways to come into an intimate and living connection with it. Some other ways to describe the spine of the character are, **"the chief motivation"** or, **"the deeper wish."** So, the spine is the character's **active response** to her or his own desires. That's worth repeating—The spine is the character's **ACTIVE RESPONSE** to his or her own deeply held desires. Every character wants something and then will do things to satisfy that want. In fact, everything the character does, is related to their deeper wish. And, personally, I love the phrase "deeper wish" because just in saying it to myself, I immediately get the feeling of a "longing for," a "passion for," of a "reaching towards." The phrase "deeper wish" is in itself, active, and most importantly, it makes clear that **the spine is not merely an intellectual hankering but a most intimate hunger.** It is utterly personal. Now certainly, this is something you and I can relate to, isn't it? This idea of the spine isn't just some technique made up for acting textbooks, it's wholly human.

Please turn to the writing exercise on the following page.

*I ask that you take a look at the things you have done in your life, the things you are doing now in your life and the things you want and hope to do in your life. When you have taken some time to give this some thought, I want you to use this page to write about your own "spine." What is your **"deeper wish"** that propels you into the things you have done, are doing and hope to do in the future. Don't rush to any conclusions. Each time you come up with something as a possibility, ask yourself again "...and why do I want to do that?"*

_____
_____
_____
_____
_____
_____
_____
_____
_____
_____
_____
_____
_____
_____
_____
_____
_____
_____

Now, let's say that as you began reading this section of the book called "WANT," and as you turned to the writing exercise and began thinking about your own past and present actions, as well as your hopes for the future, and as you were busy writing about your own "spine" until you put down your pen—let's say that all of this is a play. It's a play and you are the main character in it. The play began when you picked the book up to read and the play ended when you put down your pen after writing. **Now, did you "the character" come from nowhere, suddenly spring to life as you picked up this book and began "the play?" Did you then dissolve into nothing after you put the pen down and concluded "the play?"** Of course not. You have come from a whole lifetime of things you have done and have wanted to do, you did all the things you did just now in this "play" and, after you put the pen down, you will go off into the rest of your life which will be filled with the things you do and hope to do—and all of it is directly related to your own very specific and very personal deeper wish. The same is true of every character in every play. Although we only have the actual information provided to us by the play, we must view the character as a human being who has come from a whole life before the particular circumstances of the play occur and who will go off into the rest of his or her "life" after the play ends. We might call this the character's **"essential throughline."**

Now what do we do about this whole idea of "spine?" Hold on to that question. I'll be addressing it specifically in the next few chapters. So, let's continue…

2. RIGHT NOW!

Everything in the play must be "right now." It doesn't matter if the character is reminiscing about a failed romance or looking forward to getting married, the actor must look at everything that the character says and does as being **specifically purposeful in the present**.

(Highlight that word "specific" for yourself. It is clearly one of the most important words in the actors vocabulary! Remember this—the only way in is through specificity. Anything left general will result in acting that is general. What do I mean by general? Another word for general would be "illustrative." And acting must never be the illustration of anything, it must always be the actual experience of something. And I am telling you right now that the only path to true experience for the actor, is through the gate of specificity.)

One of my wonderful acting teachers, Suzanne Shepherd, always told us that the answer to the question "What time is it?" if you are an actor, is always "Right Now!" So, we now know that the character is doing whatever it takes to get what he wants and each thing he does, he wants to accomplish right now. Not tomorrow, not next week, RIGHT NOW!

Why "right now" you may ask...

3. THE STAKES!

When I talked with you about the characters "want," one of the first things I said is that what the character wants is always personally meaningful to them. How meaningful? **EXTREMELY MEANINGFUL!** This means that the stakes are always high and when the stakes are high, everything we do is filled with a sense of urgency. Isn't this true? Imagine sitting in your living room with your lover and watching a video together. Suddenly, the whole house shakes, the television clicks off, you hear plates falling to the floor in the kitchen and you see a painting fall off of the wall. Then, there is a huge explosion of sound and the walls cave in on top of you. Somehow, you are not seriously injured and you manage to crawl out from the wreckage, alone. You see the shocking sight of the rubble which was once your home and lots of smoke. Then, you hear a faint cry from somewhere under the remains of your house. It's your lover, still alive! Do you imagine you would be casual about saving her or his life? Or, might you have a sense of urgency in taking action? Pretty obvious, right?

Please write about a time when there was something extremely meaningful that you wanted to accomplish or have happen; when the stakes were very high. What was your deep need and what was your "active response" to this need? What did you do? How did you do it? Write in as much detail as you can, BE SPECIFIC!

_____

_____

_____

_____

_____

_____

_____

_____

_____

_____

_____

_____

_____

_____

I'll tell you two words that do not go together in any way, shape or form—"casual" and "theatre." Do you get that? There is nothing casual about anything in any well-written play. And if it's a poorly written script and you have to act it? It's still your job to make it everything but casual. *"But,"* you say, *"they are just sitting around having a casual conversation."* I am telling you that no character is just sitting around making conversation. Every character speaks words only because he or she is involved in the pursuit of something essential. **ESSENTIAL!**

○ ○ ○

So how does this all add up?

All characters in plays are human beings who want something. What they want is, in a very personal way, extremely meaningful. It is essential to them. And because the stakes are high, with a tremendous sense of urgency they actively attempt to accomplish that which will bring them closer to fulfilling their deep desire.

I gave you the two speeches from SAVAGE IN LIMBO because they are such good examples of all the dramatic elements we have been discussing. I will be using these speeches as examples as we explore, in the following chapters, some ways in which we take the written words and bring them to life.

I ask that you go back now and take another look at the two speeches from SAVAGE IN LIMBO. For each speech, I want you to write down some notes about the things we've just been talking about: What does each character want and how high are the stakes? On the following page, please do that now.

"True creativity often starts where language ends."
Arthur Koestler

"It's not the words you say, it's the music you play."

Let me ask you something. When you began to respond to the questions in this last writing exercise, where did you go first? This isn't a trick question, you probably went to the **words** spoken by each of the characters. For us actors, **the Script is our Bible.** Let's slow down and look at what I just said. "The Script is our Bible." Now, whether you believe the Bible to be the account of actual historical events, or as a purely fictitious group of books, or maybe you are somewhere in between—whichever —clearly, the Bible presents the stories of many characters, each living in a specific time and place, saying things and doing things, in relationship with others and struggling through momentous circumstances and events. **But what is the Bible's purpose?** (You may not be into the Bible yourself. If not, imagine, for a few moments, what it might be for those who are.) The Bible has been called the "light of truth" and we can certainly say that the Bible's purpose is in the arena of "spirit" and "inspiration." Let's go to the dictionary for a moment—

Inspire: To fill with enlivening or exalting emotion.
To stimulate to action.
To affect or touch.
To draw forth; elicit or arouse.
To be the cause or source of.
To stimulate energies.

Spirit: The vital principle or animating force within living beings.
The part of a human being associated with the mind, will and feelings.

The essential nature of a person.
The actual though unstated sense or significance
of something.

Two powerful words, and directly related to the relationship between the actor and the script. Don't you think? And so, we must open ourselves to the play. And, in terms of choosing the best material to work on, we know we have found a good match when the literal or the "facts" given to us by the playwright "touch our essential nature"; when the facts given to us by the playwright "arouse our mind, will and feelings." For the facts given to us by the playwright must serve as the springboard for our creative imagination and they must "stimulate us to action." Now we have a shot at bringing soul to the stage. My favorite description of soul comes from John Bradshaw, who said that the soul is, *"That which in us is most human."* Because, LISTEN NOW, (I'm gonna make a big point here) LISTEN NOW, ACTING IS NEVER ABOUT THE WORDS!

You may say, *"That's strange. The play is a bunch of words and I have to speak those words. Whaddya mean acting is not about the words?"* What I mean is that real acting is always about that which makes the words come out of your mouth. Just as it is about that which makes it impossible to talk. Or, that which makes you whisper cautiously, or scream in delight, or jump for joy, etc...If we flash back to one of the definitions I mentioned for the word spirit, we find a useful thought: **Real Acting is always about the "actual though unstated significance of something."** I would also add the word **"unseen"** to go along with **"unstated"** because everything we end up seeing on stage, when the acting is alive, is really the result of that which is unseen. So what the audience gets are both the story being told by the words and, more importantly, the story that is **actually happening** while the words are being spoken.

I would like you to think back and remember a significant moment in your life from a good number of years ago. Take some time to close your eyes and go over the details of this event. What do you remember? Use this page to write about all the details of the event as specifically as you can.

_____

_____

_____

_____

_____

_____

_____

_____

_____

_____

_____

_____

_____

_____

_____

_____

_____

_____

_____

_____

_____

_____

You know, I can think back to many important and power-ful moments in my life. And when I do, I remember so many details: the look in the other person's eyes, something physical that they did, what was happening in our environment, how I felt inside, the colors and smells and sounds, etc...But, the one thing I can rarely remember, are any of the words. I remember almost nothing or not a thing about what was actually spoken. The same is true for the audience when they leave the play, most of the words of the play will fade pretty fast. But if the acting was authentic and alive, those who witnessed it may have moments of the performance stick with them for life.

○　○　○

I want to introduce you to a way of starting to work with the script. So...

Let's go back to the speeches from *SAVAGE IN LIMBO*. After spending your initial time with the script, allowing the words to freely do what they do to you, the next step is to write down whatever strikes you as the most provocative things the character says. These words, as you start to write them down, will begin to give you a more defined picture of how the char-acter views his world, what he wants and how badly he wants it. When you write these statements down, it is important that you use the character's actual words and not what you think the character means by what he is saying. Here is what I would write down as I examine the speeches of Tony and Savage:

Tony—
I always went for the girl like you. And what finally fuckin come to me, what finally fuckin penetrated the wall here, was there was somethin else. Somethin I never even thought about, didn't have a clue about.

There's other people. Like in science fiction. Another dimension right there but you can't see it. I got into it for a minute by accident. Through a crack. I caught a flash.

I'm like one a those guys inna factory and they bring in all new machines. That's what I feel like. Like I gotta retrain or I'm gonna lose my place.

I wanna see the things I didn't see before an let the stuff I was lookin at go by.

I wanna look at somethin else. I wanna know somethin else. I'm thirty-two years old. I wanna change.

○   ○   ○

Savage—
We're on the cliff.

Ain't you tired a livin if this is all livin is?

This is not life. This is not life. This is not life.

God, gimme somethin else cause this is definitely not it. New eyes new ears new hands. Gimme back my soul from where you took it, gimme back my friends, gimme back my priests an my father, and take this goddamn virginity from off my life.

HUNGER HUNGER HUNGER.

If somebody don't give me somethin, I'm gonna die.

It's like I'm some woman lives inna cave and plays with stones.

You can't keep up your courage alone, playin with stones.

○ ○ ○

Those are the words that really do something to me. You can see that I left out most of the "story" and I narrowed the speeches down to what are, to me, the most provocative statements. So, what do you do with them now that you have them written down? At this stage, all there is to do is to allow them to work on you. Don't come to any big conclusions about anything yet. You see, if you take these statements and say them over and over to yourself, they are going to do something to you. And what they do to you, is personal. Listen, we are planting seeds. Do you get that, we are planting seeds right now. Here, try this:

I want you to take these words from Savage, **"If somebody don't give me somethin, I'm gonna die."** *First, I ask that you close your eyes and spend a few minutes just saying those words over and over to yourself—not out loud. Say that sentence over and over and see how it starts to affect you. As you open your eyes, go to the top of the following page and,* **1. Write the sentence down and then, 2. Continue writing out of your experience of those words.** *Allow your writing to be a* **free association.** *Do not censor anything and do not pause to think of what to write.* **Keep writing until you have filled the following two pages.**

_____

_____

_____

_____

_____

_____

_____

_____

_____

_____

_____

_____

_____

_____

_____

_____

_____

_____

_____

_____

_____

_____

_____

_____

_____

What we just did in the exercise is start to bring you and the playwright's words together. The act of locating the provocative statements, writing them down, saying them to ourselves in a quiet and relaxed manner and then writing our responses down, is a wonderful way to start knocking at the door of the characters **"point of view."** And as we continue to work in this way, along with some of the other things I will be sharing with you, that door will soon open for us to enter.

There are the words on the page which came from the life of the playwright and from what the playwright knows. Somehow, the actor must find his and her way into those words so that the words now come from the life of the actor and what the actor knows. Which brings us to the next chapter...

chapter 2

Acting with Meaning

"There can be no knowledge without emotion. We may be aware of a truth, yet until we have felt its force, it is not ours. To the cognition of the brain must be added the experience of the soul."

Arnold Bennett

Just a few days ago, we held very early, general auditions for a play I would like to do next year at my theatre here in Seattle. This is a production that we will produce only if we are able to find the right cast. If we do the play, I will be acting in it and I will have the opportunity to be directed by someone I am very interested in working with. In the four hours of auditions, the director and I saw over fifty actors. The actors were asked to come in and do a contemporary monologue and to be prepared to read from the script. Now, first of all, during the auditions, nearly half of the actors told us that they had not read the play we were holding auditions for and they did not know what the play was about. Did you hear that? This is a well-known, published play, and at least half of the actors did not know what the play they were auditioning for was about! I'll tell you, Zip-Boom-Bang, they just blew their shot.

The main thing I wanted to tell you about those auditions is that as the actors came in and did their monologues, a majority of those actors did not know what they were talking about. I am saying that as they performed their monologues, they did not know what they were talking about. This was not unusual, it was sadly typical. And when I watch actors who don't know what they are talking about, whether it's watching actors in an audition or watching actors in a play, my attention will naturally go to something more interesting—getting some new paint on that wall over there, thinking about my children, etc....This aspect of acting, "knowing what you're talking about" and the topic of the next chapter, "knowing what you are doing," are the two things I have seen as most missing in the large majority of actors' work. Without them, of course, there is no real acting going on.

What exactly do I mean by "knowing what you're talking about?" I'll get into it in this way...

In a workshop I did many years ago, the instructor said something fantastic to us, though at the time it totally baffled me and made me mad. He said, *"Life is empty and meaningless."* My inner response to that was, "Who the hell are you? How dare you tell me my life is empty and meaningless!" It took me quite a while to understand what he was talking about, or at least come to what I think he was talking about. What I believe he was saying was that **life itself** is empty in that it is the "container," a kind of wide open realm of possibility. And, that it is meaningless, or without meaning, until we invest it with meaning. There are two old Zen quotes I hand out to my "in person" students which speak to this:

We shape clay into a pot
but it is the emptiness inside
that holds whatever we want.

We hammer wood for a house
but it is the inner space
that makes it livable.

Are you humming the theme song from *The Twilight Zone* by now? If this is starting to sound a little too mysterious, well it is. Acting, ultimately, is mysterious. You know, technique is really about giving oneself a kind of structure which will encourage the unexplainable to occur. Remember, we are talking about real acting here; we are talking about taking the words off of a piece of paper and breathing life into them; we are talking about an act of creation—which is always mysterious. So, we can take the statement that "life is empty and meaningless" and apply it to our acting. Our acting is empty and meaningless until we bring it to life by first, injecting it with meaning.

And when I say **"know"** in the "know what you're talking about," I'm not talking about any kind of intellectual concept you may have about the character or what he says. I'm also not talking about your mastery of any facts that you might look up in an encyclopedia. Here, let me get more specific—

Please turn to the writing exercise on the following page:

Please use this page to write about an experience from your childhood. Choose to write about either a wonderful event that involved you and a family member or an unpleasant event that involved you and a family member. Please do that now.

_____

_____

_____

_____

_____

_____

_____

_____

_____

_____

_____

_____

_____

_____

_____

_____

_____

_____

_____

_____

_____

As you wrote down your childhood experience just now, where did the words come from? If the writing about it did something to you, where did those responses come from? If it brought images to mind, where did those images come from? I say, It all came from your "knowing"; from what you really know. Now, where is this "knowing" do you think? Where is it located? Here is something that happened to me when I was five years old:

I was playing in a neighbor's yard with a friend and we were near the lady's flowers. I didn't see that the flower bed was enclosed with a very low and spiked metal fence. As we were playing, I got pushed and I fell backwards onto the flowers. We were scared that the lady would come out and yell at us, so we got onto our bikes and took off. While I was riding, I felt something on my head. I reached up to see what was in my hair and it was very wet and thick. When I brought my hand down, it was totally red. It took me a moment to realize that my hand was all bloody, which meant that my head was bleeding! Terrified, I zoomed home and my parents rushed me to the hospital to get my head stitched up.

Now, when I recall that story and I flash back to the moment I reached up to my head and felt that it was all wet, I notice my right arm stiffens up. I still experience in my chest the shock and the fear of the moment when I saw my right hand and it was covered with blood. I still feel the pressure in my legs as I lifted my behind off of the seat of the bike so I could push harder on the pedals to get home faster. This whole event, even after all these years, is still alive and present in my body, in my muscles, in my gut and my mind and heart. And if you were here with me and I was telling you that story, you'd notice that I don't really have to "think" about it. The words simply emerge on their own as I am talking with you because I am talking about something I really know and which has true meaning to me.

What you must realize is that the same is true for every character in every play. The characters are talking from something they really know and which has true meaning to them. Like when Tony talks about the transformational experience of being with the ugly girl or when Savage talks about the horrendous loneliness of playing pool by herself, they are talking from personal experience. THEY KNOW WHAT THEY ARE TALKING ABOUT.

Now we are faced with a huge challenge, right? Those things that the characters are talking about happened to them, not to us. And those specific experiences have personal meaning to them, not to us. Yet, it is our job to live out the circumstances of the play "as if" they were true for US. (As Sanford Meisner taught us, acting is "living truthfully under imaginary circumstances.") In other words, if you are to live truthfully on stage, you must be inside those words you speak. **YOU** have to be in those words. Not some interesting idea of "the character." **YOU** must be in those words because when you are on stage, YOU ARE THE CHARACTER.

The kind of knowing we have talked about so far, has been dealing with the personal history of the character; events and relationships of both the past and the present. And I have been leading to the fact that we have to, somehow, make those experiences our own so that when we speak those words on stage, they come from our own knowing. The way I have seen many acting classes deal with this, especially in the colleges, is to have actors create a "biography" of the character. The teacher has the actor make up a biography that includes all kinds of intellectually interesting facts about the character's past that the actor might not find in the script. For the most part, this effort has absolutely no value because it does not help the actor act the part. It merely gives you lots of useless information to try and juggle around in your brain. This brings to mind a quote:

> *"Depend upon it, there comes a time when for every addition of knowledge you forget something that you knew before. It is of the highest importance, therefore, not to have useless facts elbowing out the useful ones."*
> Sir Arthur Conan Doyle

I will soon show you a way to build a personal history for the character that springs from the character and you at the same time; that brings you and the character into an intimate connectedness; that, as we have talked about, enables you to speak the words from the script out of your own true knowing. Before I do that, I want to go back to a subject I have introduced and which must be grappled with, and that is the character's **point of view**.

I want you to get today's newspaper. Cut out an article that really makes you angry. When you read it, it makes your blood boil! Tape the article on the following page and write about your responses to the article.

tape article here

write about article here

_____

_____

_____

_____

_____

_____

_____

_____

_____

_____

_____

_____

_____

_____

_____

_____

_____

_____

_____

_____

_____

_____

_____

Go back to the newspaper and find an article that excites you or makes you want to jump for joy or proud to be a member of the human race! Tape the article on this page and on the following page, write your responses to the article.

tape article here

write about article here

_____
_____
_____
_____
_____
_____
_____
_____
_____
_____
_____
_____
_____
_____
_____
_____
_____
_____
_____
_____
_____
_____
_____
_____
_____
_____

What do you think we were doing with the newspaper articles? If you say it has to do with point of view, you're right. I was asking you to start to take a look at your own point of view, at what pushes your own buttons. "Point of view" is how we assign meaning to everything and everyone around us, it is how we look out towards the world and the attitudes with which we receive and respond to the world. We can say that one's character is really defined by his or her point of view because it is this specific point of view that, ultimately, determines one's behavior. (It's my own belief that, as an actor, you must get very clear on your own point of view and to be constantly curious about the points of view of others.) And so, as we have discussed the need to make personal the events and relationships in the character's life, you must also come into an inner alignment with the character's point of view. Only then is it possible for you to behave authentically through the "eyes" of the character and for the character to come to life in a most vivid way.

Before I get into working on the kind of "personalization" we've been talking about, I want to make something I mentioned at the beginning of this chapter, very clear. Now, you could certainly work on a monologue for an audition and not read the play—but why would you want to? I just don't get why anyone would not be interested enough to get the play and read it. I don't get how anyone who is that lazy dares to think the theatre holds a place for them. Of course, I see this all the time, which is why I am bothering to talk about something so obvious. It's one thing if you are doing a piece that really stands on it's own. But the rest of the time, the monologue lives in the context of the scene and of the play and without reading the play you remain ignorant of SO MUCH! Of course, what you will be oblivious to is crucial information that will directly impact how you do the monologue.

For example: In the Savage speech we're working with, at one point Savage implores God to *take this goddamn virginity from off my life.* Without reading the play, how would you begin to approach that line? Without reading the play, you'd have to wonder what she really means—is she talking about virginity literally in terms of sexual experience, or is she talking about the kind of emotional isolation she lives in? If you found the speech in a book of monologues for actors, they would probably tell you in the introduction to the speech that she really is a thirty-two-year-old virgin, that she has never been with a man. But is that enough for you, the actor? No, you still must read the play, you must! In the play, you discover that Savage talks very specifically about her virginity, not simply as a sexual issue, but as a manifestation of a complex and profound current that colors every aspect of her existence. From the play, you'd have the gift of the provocative images and thoughts Savage shares with Linda in lines such as, *"I'm talkin about tension. I'm talkin about somethin snappin at your heels, but you can't get away. Bein apart from everybody else. Bein alone. There's a wall there. Like you're inna glass box, a bee inna jar, dreamin about flowers, smellin your own...death. People look at you, it's through somethin. You touch somebody, there's somethin over your hand."*

And there's much more! But my main point is, do your homework and read the play. This is just so obvious, isn't it. I mean, if nothing else, imagine the director stopping you and asking why you chose this piece, what you love about the play and to tell him or her more about the character. Here's another way you better be prepared and "know what you are talking about" because, I'll tell you, if you're not prepared, not interested enough to go the extra mile, there is a stack of pictures and resumes on that director's desk of actors who are READY AND HUNGRY to work.

In our acting we are always doing one of two things:

- **we are either talking about what we know,**
   or
- **we are showing what we don't know.**

Okay, let's go.

*As we did in Chapter One with the two monologues from SAV-AGE IN LIMBO, I now want you to go through the entire play and write a list of provocative statements made by Tony and Savage that clue you in to their **point of view**. (Provocative to who? To You!) Also, don't limit yourself to what the characters say, take a good look at anything they do that interests you. For example, the owner of the bar, Murk, waters the dead plants. When Savage asks him, "Murk, why you water those plants? They're dead." Murk says, "They don't know that." Hmmm…that's an interesting point of view, don't you think? So get to work investigating. Remember, in this list use the actual words of the character, not what you conjecture or think they might mean by what they say. (If you haven't read the play by now, please read the play at least one time and then come back here to do the writing on the following pages.)*

Tony

_____

_____

_____

_____

_____

_____

_____

_____

_____

_____

_____

_____

_____

_____

_____

_____

_____

_____

_____

_____

_____

_____

_____

_____

_____

_____

_____

Tony

_____

_____

_____

_____

_____

_____

_____

_____

_____

_____

_____

_____

_____

_____

_____

_____

_____

_____

_____

_____

_____

_____

_____

Savage

_____
_____
_____
_____
_____
_____
_____
_____
_____
_____
_____
_____
_____
_____
_____
_____
_____
_____
_____
_____
_____
_____
_____
_____
_____
_____
_____

Savage

_____

_____

_____

_____

_____

_____

_____

_____

_____

_____

_____

_____

_____

_____

_____

_____

_____

_____

_____

_____

_____

_____

_____

_____

_____

_____

_____

Now that you have the list, if you were actually working on either of these characters towards an audition, I would ask that you spend some time each day just saying those statements over and over to yourself. Not doing anything with them, just allowing them to work on you. And as we did in Chapter One, you might then choose to freely write down your responses. And as those words are "brewing" in you, we may now go on to another part of your homework—building the personal "history" that unites you and the character. To do this I want to introduce you to what I call the **"Key Facts."**

The **key facts** include any person, place or thing the character speaks about that has meaning to him or her. I call them key facts because they do not include every fact, just the ones you think are of some importance to the character. For example, when Savage comes into the bar at the beginning of the play, she tells Murk that "I just ate two Cornish game hens and a buncha broccoli." Well, I wouldn't consider the hens and the broccoli to be key facts. Right after that though, Savage does give us a couple of key facts, she says "I can't sit in that apartment that smells like a catbox with my mother who looks like a dead walrus for one more second or I will die." The "apartment" and the "mother" are two things I would want to know more about for myself, and I will soon show you a specific way to get at that. And once more, the purpose here? Our aim is to, eventually, arrive at the place where the words you speak come from what **you really know**.

Since I have shared the story of my falling backwards and the metal spike putting a hole in my head, here's an example. Let's say I was shopping at Home Depot with my wife and she said, *"Honey, look at the sale on metal spikes. We can put them around the flower bed and keep that big grey cat out."* And I turn to her and say, *"There's no way in hell I'm putting any metal spikes*

in our yard, near our house, or near the kids. There's NO WAY!"
Now, when I say "metal spikes," I don't have to go into the story
about falling on them when I was five, I don't even have to think
about that event. Those words come out of my mouth filled
with my own specific relationship and history with those metal
spikes—I know what I'm talking about.

Now, imagine you are cast in a new full-length play called
WATCH OUT FOR THE FLOWERS! and you got the lead part
of Barry, a talented young author who is involved in a tremendous struggle to meet the deadline on his newest book—a book
he calls "Loving The Condition." In the first act, you/Barry have
a scene with the character who is your wife. Here are your lines:

Julia: Honey, look at the sale on metal spikes. We can put
them around the flower bed and keep that big grey cat out.
    Barry: There's no way in hell I'm putting any metal spikes in
our yard, near our house, or near the kids. There's NO WAY!

Now let's say that in act two of *Watch Out For The Flowers!*,
Barry apologizes to Julia for blowing up at her about the spikes.
This leads him into a monologue about falling on a metal spike
near a flower bed when he was a kid. He speaks about how the
spike nearly killed him and how he ran from the woman neighbor who he thought would scream at him for harming some of
her flowers. He shares how that event scared him away from ever
being in a relationship with a woman who likes to grow flowers;
how he was, at the same time, always most attracted to women
who wanted to grow flowers; how the traumatic event led him
into ten years of psychoanalysis, starting a national support
group for men who have a fear of women who love gardening,
trying to have a new law enacted that would end the use of
metal spikes for the protection of gardens—all of which is the
personal journey he talks about in his new book, "Loving The

Condition." (Hey, what do you think—do I have any chance at becoming a playwright?...Uh,...well then, how about a stand-up comic? No? Oh well.)

Well, that monologue certainly gives you a deeper understanding of Barry and his relationship with the metal spikes. But even out of the two-line exchange between Julia and Barry in "act one," you know two very important things about Barry and the metal spikes. One, you know Barry has strong feelings about metal spikes and two, you know that he doesn't want them around his home and family. But the truth of the matter is that you the actor couldn't care less about metal spikes, they mean nothing to you. Your challenge and your mission, should you choose to accept it, is to make the metal spikes mean something to you. And guided by how you know Barry feels about them, it is clear that you must get yourself to the place where you too do not want metal spikes near you or those you love. Well, how do we begin to integrate the key facts into our own knowing? Before we get into that...

I want you to go back to SAVAGE IN LIMBO *and go through the play two times. The first time through, write down the Key Facts for Tony—everything that Tony says that you think will be important to "make your own." On the second time through, write down everything that Savage says that you would want to "make your own." Please use the following pages for your lists of key facts. Please do this before continuing to read this book.*

Tony

_____
_____
_____
_____
_____
_____
_____
_____
_____
_____
_____
_____
_____
_____
_____
_____
_____
_____
_____
_____
_____
_____
_____
_____
_____
_____
_____

Savage

_____

_____

_____

_____

_____

_____

_____

_____

_____

_____

_____

_____

_____

_____

_____

_____

_____

_____

_____

_____

_____

_____

_____

_____

_____

_____

_____

Here are some of the key facts that I wrote down:

Tony—

My car
The ugly girl
Linda
The girl like you
The old flicks
My routine (the girl the car and the bed)
Jimmy Rina
Having a son

Savage—

Scales
The jukebox
Murk
My apartment
My mother
Cotters
The P.C.
Playin pool
Linda
Tony Aronica
I'm a virgin
love
My job
Dancin
April
My dream
My friends
My priests
My father

Did you write most of those down? You know, sometimes the key facts jump out at you and sometimes they are less obvious. For example, I wrote down "having a son" as a key fact for Tony. Why? It is late in the play that Tony finds out from Linda that he has a child. His first response is, *"WHAT?"* He's clearly shocked. And then he finds out it's a son and the son has a name—Alphonse. Now, it's not so much in what Tony says that led me to choose "having a son" as one of the key facts, it's more what he starts to do. The first really interesting thing to me is that soon after he hears about the boy Alphonse, Tony shuts up for a while. Savage and Murk go on talking about other things, but the next thing Tony says to Linda is, *"I have a son?"* It's clear he has been thinking about this incredible news. I say, Tony experiences being moved in an unexpected and powerful way. Now what leads me to that belief? Well first, Tony goes on to get more information about Alphonse and he wants to know if Linda can get him back. But the real core of my interpretation is that it is the news about Alphonse that leads Tony to make a huge and revolutionary decision, *"Then we'll get a place an we'll live together seven days the week."* And part of the new picture of life for Tony is having his son, *"You wanna claim that kid or what?"* Even the last thing Tony says in the play is the name of his son, *"Alphonse."* But don't think that that's some kind of sentimental ending of the play for Tony. I believe that what he is really saying in his last line is something like, "Now why would you go and give my boy such a crummy name?" And where do you think I got that impression from? Listen, I don't make things up, I always go to my Bible—the script! If you recall, when Tony first hears that his son was named Alphonse, he and Linda have this exchange:

TONY: His name's Alphonse?
LINDA: Yup
TONY: Who named him that?

LINDA: Me
TONY: And does it like, stick?
LINDA: Yeah, it sticks. It's his name.

You might find other meanings in those lines, that's perfectly fine. Just be sure that the choices you make are always based in the script.

Now a key fact like "the ugly girl" for Tony is a much easier one to spot because we know from the monologue we have looked at that his encounter with the ugly girl was completely transformational for him—it has given him a hunger to *"see the things I didn't see before an let the stuff I was lookin at go by."* And it has given him a determination to *"go against my life with everything I got. I'm gonna attack my fuckin self as I am...And I am majorly majorly gonna change."*

Are you starting to see the kind of investigative work we are involved in? I think this kind of working with the script is tremendously fun. It is certainly essential. And remember, even though you might only be doing a monologue from the play, your in-depth work on the entire play will have a big payoff for you.

Let's move on now, I want to show you a specific way to work with the key facts that you have written down. The first thing you do, once you have the key facts, is to write each one down on the top of a blank page in a journal or notebook that is devoted to your working on the play. I will give you the blank pages here in the book to work on, but normally, I would ask that you have a notebook devoted solely to your work on the character you are going to play. After you have written one key fact at the top of each page, go back to the play and then, under each key fact, write everything that the character says that is related to that fact. Always use the character's actual words. For example, if you were working on the part of Savage, at the top of one page you would write this key fact for Savage:

Murk

(and then under Murk you would write what Savage says about him:)

Let it sit up there a minute. It drives him crazy. It drives him nuts. It preys on his mind.

He's never grown up. He still thinks he's playin Simon Says in the playground.

You can't take no back and forth at all.

...and you would continue to find whatever else Savage says in the play that is related to Murk and write it on this page.

You will also find that sometimes the character may mention some of the key facts only once in the play, so there are no other lines of information to write under them. (Like when Savage mentions her father in the monologue we've been looking at.) That's all right, if you consider them important facts, you would still put each one at the top of a page. Let's do this now...

Right now, I want you to take any three of the key facts from your lists. Choose three that interest you and which you would like to do some work with. Put one key fact at the top of each of the following three blank pages. Then go to the play and under each of the key facts, write anything that the character says throughout the play, related to that fact. (Also, write as small as you can so room remains on each page.) Please do that now before continuing to read this book.

Key Fact _____

_____

_____

_____

_____

_____

_____

_____

_____

_____

_____

_____

_____

_____

_____

_____

_____

_____

_____

Key Fact _____

_____

_____

_____

_____

_____

_____

_____

_____

_____

_____

_____

_____

_____

_____

_____

_____

_____

_____

_____

_____

_____

_____

_____

_____

_____

_____

Key Fact _____

_____
_____
_____
_____
_____
_____
_____
_____
_____
_____
_____
_____
_____
_____
_____
_____
_____
_____
_____
_____
_____
_____

All right, let's continue. Out of your readings of the play, your exploring the character's point of view and what you have just done with the three key facts you chose, you have a good idea about how the character thinks and feels about each of these facts. The next thing we are going to do with each key fact is begin to make them more specifically related to you.

I find that the **COMBINATION** of 1) allowing our imagination to lead us without judging or censoring ourselves, and 2) the act of actually writing the words down on paper, with our fingers and a pen, as the words are coming to us—is a powerful union. For me, and for many actors I have worked with, the writing it down somehow helps to plant our thoughts, feelings and images in us and they take root in a deeper way. And so, we are now going to continue writing where we left off with each key fact. And what we will be writing will be **a free association, guided by the attitude of the character about that key fact**. I'll say that again. We will be writing down our free association, which means that we will be writing as we give free reign to our imagination. And, our imagination will be guided by the attitudes and feelings of the character towards the key fact we are working with.

And importantly, **we will be writing in first person.**

We are not writing about the character or as the character.

We are writing **as ourselves** about the key fact, **guided by the attitudes of the character.**

For example, if we were working with Tony and his key fact "the ugly girl," it is clear to us that he is deeply shaken by the experience of being with her. We know that:

...the experience was totally unusual and new for Tony...

"And do you know something? It was the best. It was the best I ever had. And it whadn't cause she knew a lotta tricks or like that. It was cause she'd told me about the Soviet Union. And then she left. Now here's the thing. She was very ugly. I don't even wanna talk about how she looked. Mucho ugly. I didn't think I could ever be with a woman like that. But it came about outta whatever, happenstance, and I was. And it turned out to be better than what I went after."

...out of what happened between them, Tony is opened to the fact that there are possibilities for living that he was never aware of...

"I always went for the girl like you. And what finally fuckin come to me, what finally fuckin penetrated the wall here, was there was somethin else. Somethin I never even thought about, didn't have a clue about. When I talked to you, I called it ugly girls. I don't know what to call it. There's other people. Like in science fiction. Another dimension right there but you can't see it. I got into it for a minute by accident. Through a crack. I caught a flash. The dimension a ugly girls."

...he realizes he has frittered away his life...

"Waste. It's like I wish they froze me inna block a ice till it was time and I was ready to make my move so I didn't waste anything. Waste, right? You clowns know about waste. I know about waste. I fuckin invented waste."

…he feels a sense of urgency about making something new happen…

"I wanna look at somethin else. I wanna know somethin else. I'm thirty-two years old. I wanna change." And, *"What the fuck, did you think you were gonna live forever? You're not. Stand up. It's pissin away. Your life."*

So after writing "The ugly girl" at the top of a page and writing underneath it all the things Tony says related to his experience with the ugly girl, we would continue with—*our own imaginative writing in first person guided by Tony's point of view toward this encounter.* Now, **what you must not do**, is try to make all the things Tony says appear in some way in your writing. If you do that, your head gets in the way of the part of you that has new information available about that event. What we have to do, is be open to what we get. The more you do this work, the more surprised you will be at the ease in which your imagination offers you new and personal information about each key fact. Here's what a free association about the ugly girl might look like:

why did she step into my life and shake me up I was comfortably ignorant and now I can never get back but thank God she did because I was dying inside and now my blood is surging through my veins for the first time I want to scream I want to run and yell and wake up the neighbors I AM ALIVE she looked in my eyes and her eyes were burning I have never seen such big blue eyes so blue like the sea and if I moved away from her for a moment she held my hand and whispered in my ear it's all right you have the ability to love and to be a powerful force in your world and she kissed the back of my hand and said love she kissed it again and said love that's all she said just love and then she disappeared she vanished I want her back I want to know more I want to touch her and understand I want her strength I don't want to go on the way I have scared and small I want to play big I want to make something mean something I want to hear her whisper again and smell her breath it smelled like oranges sweet and tangy I don't know where she came from or where she went...

Well, there's a sample for you. Now I have started to make the event with the ugly girl, **my** event with the ugly girl. Now when I say the words "ugly girl," I know that she has burning blue eyes and that she kissed the back of my hand. I know that she whispered into my ear and that her breath smelled like oranges. Because my imagination created those things, those things are mine. And as I said, somehow the writing it down adds to my own connection to what I have discovered. I have started to build my own relationship with the ugly girl. And "build" is a good word because we are forging something here. We are not yet concerned with any kind of finished product or how these "key facts" will show up in our acting. If we really do this aspect of the work, we can trust that our personal connection to the words **will** show up in our acting; it will show up in our **"behavior"** on stage and it will happen on its own. What do I mean by that? Well, let me use the "spike story" one more time. If I said to you, *"When I was a kid I had a nasty accident with a metal spike,"* my hand might, on its own, go up and touch the spot on my head where I was injured. Now, in that statement, *"When I was a kid I had a nasty accident with a metal spike,"* I didn't even mention yet that the spike went into my head and I certainly didn't stop to think, *"Hey, if I touch my head in this interesting way, this person will really believe this happened to me."* (It is only bad actors who think, *"Hey, if I do this or that in this interesting way, the audience will really believe this happened to me."* They have to SHOW because they don't really KNOW!) As I said, my hand going to my head, this "BEHAVIOR," happened on its own and **effortlessly** because I know what I am talking about.

Let me relate this to my own imaginative writing on the "ugly girl" page. If I were doing the Tony monologue, without even noticing it or deciding to do it, I might raise my fist and point out the back of my hand to Linda as I'm saying *"She started rappin to me about the Soviet Union."* That might happen because in my writing on the key fact page, I discovered that the ugly girl kissed me there. I didn't try to make that physical gesture happen, it just did. Now, we are starting to fill the words with "that which is unstated and unseen." I may decide later not to point to my fist, or the director may say he doesn't want me to do that, but at least there is the beginnings of a life brewing in me and in my relationship to what I'm talking about.

By the time you act the part, you must know more than anybody about the character—more than the director and more than the playwright. Also, you can be creative in many ways with your work on the key facts. If you were playing Tony, you might want to cut out a picture from a magazine to tape onto the "ugly girl" page so you know what the ugly girl looks like specifically. If you find powerful connections to music, it would be great to choose a song that was playing on the car radio when the "ugly girl" got into your car. You could tell a friend to put something in your car that might drop out of a woman's purse and not to tell you what it is. Then, when you find it in your car, you can say that it was left behind by the "ugly girl." The more you involve all of your senses and your creativity, the more personally persuasive all of this work will be; the more FUN it will be—and don't you want to have some fun?

Back to the key facts now:

I want you to go back to the three key facts you chose. Under what you have all ready written, continue to write in the kind of first person, free association we have been discussing. A free association guided by the attitudes of the character. Write until you have filled the remaining space on each page. Please do that for each key fact before continuing to read this book.

How did your writing go? Were you surprised at what you discovered? If you were actually playing the part of Tony or of Savage I would ask that you do some writing in this manner every day. You would write—not a lot, just a few new sentences—on every one of the key fact pages, each day. In this way, you would be continually deepening your personal relationship with the character and with what is meaningful to him or her. You would also see that this one approach to personalization is not an isolated part of your work on the monologue or the play, it is done in partnership with and bouncing off of all the other things you are addressing.

chapter 3

Acting with Purpose

"What you are doing" is the propellant which makes the words necessary to speak; **necessary to speak right now**. Of course, when we really know what we are doing (in speech or in silence) and then when we really do that, what occurs is much more than just words. What emerges will include the words, a whole physical life and rich human behavior. Now combine "really doing something" with "really knowing what you are talking about," well, now we've got some authentic life on this stage—which is both thrilling and rare. (And worth the price of admission!)

As in everything we have been exploring together, the kind of "doing something" on stage we are discussing is not merely some sort of interesting acting technique. It is, of course, true in life as well. In our lives, just because we rarely examine what it is we are "doing" everytime we open up our mouths and talk with someone, or while we are listening to others, that doesn't mean it isn't happening. We are always involved in "doing something," whether we are talking or not, and it is always in relation to the other person or people we are dealing with at that moment.

Sometimes, that which we are doing is directly expressed in the words we use. For example, if I had something important I was trying to say to you and you kept your eyes glued on the TV—I might take the remote control out of your hand, click off the television, take your chin in my hand, turn your face to me and say,

"I want you to listen to me and give me your undivided attention!"

So, you might call what I was doing in that moment, "demanding your complete attention." As we know from the last chapter, my need to have you give me your attention would depend on the actual importance of what it is I want to tell you. So here we see a good example of how these two elements— knowing what you're talking about and knowing what you're doing—always work hand in hand. If I didn't really have anything important to say to you, why would I bother to go as far as I went to get your attention? I wouldn't.

Now that's the problem I often see with actors—one (or many times both) of these two vital components is missing. And if one is missing, the acting has to be false. If you only deal with the personal and emotional deepening side of things, without the doing side, you end up with acting that is mushy, general, disconnected to anyone else on stage and without purpose. I have seen a lot of this kind of emotional masturbation on stage and it's not a pretty sight. If you only deal with the doing side, without coming to a specific personal relationship with why you are saying all these things, you become one of those "objective actors"; an actor who plots out his performance, going from objective to objective to objective without any real reason to do them. This "objective actor" may be slick, but he is always completely hollow. This actor is also never in real relationship with his partners on stage because if he doesn't really need to do the things he is pretending to do, how can it possibly matter what the hell anybody else on stage is doing or how they are responding to him?

I gave you an example of how sometimes what you are doing is directly expressed in the words: *"I want your undivided attention."* More often though, what we are doing is not expressed directly in the words. For example, if I was the one watching TV and it was the Sonics and they were in the final round of the playoffs and my wife kept trying to get my attention, I might say to her very sweetly and with a big kiss,

"Honey, I forgot to tell you. I brought home your favorite cheesecake. It's in the fridge—yummy, yummy, yummy!"

Now, I probably wasn't very concerned about her needs in that moment, about being a nice guy or about how happy she'd be to have her cheesecake. What I was doing was getting her off my back so I could watch the game. What's really underneath all my sweet behavior is what I want from her which is to "LEAVE ME ALONE RIGHT NOW SO I CAN WATCH THE GAME!" When we look at this example, we can see that, in one way or another, our words are always "riding on top of" that which we are really doing. Here, try this...

*For one whole day, I want you to examine the things you talk about with others and what is underneath those words—what is it that you are really doing as you are talking. Each time you have been with someone, ask yourself, "What did I want to get, what did I want to give, what did I want to accomplish?" Do not **try** to do anything extra when you are with people to make this happen, just notice what it is that you are doing. At the end of the day, go to the writing exercise on the following page.*

What kinds of things did you notice about what you were doing as you were with people in various situations? What was underneath your words and your behavior. Write as specifically as you can.

_____

_____

_____

_____

_____

_____

_____

_____

_____

_____

_____

_____

_____

_____

_____

_____

_____

_____

_____

_____

_____

I hope you will find it encouraging to know that, although the work on "doings" may be demanding and sometimes elusive, it is not foreign to us. Also, when we begin to get in touch with what it is we are doing in our daily lives, we see that we are always purposeful. Now, I'm not talking about the nature of that purpose, I'm saying that in some specific way we are always trying to accomplish something. And us humans reveal an infinite variety of behaviors: we do things that are bold, silly, cowardly, risky, wise, harmful, helpful, courageous, selfish, supportive, pushy, noble, loving and ETC! Sometimes we do things that take us closer to that which we want to achieve (a cigarette smoker may finally stop smoking because she is pregnant and she wants to care for the child growing inside her) and sometimes we do things that work totally against us (a man who is about to get married to a woman he loves, has a one night sexual affair with a stranger). Either way, and whether we want to admit it or not, we always do what we do with some specific purpose.

The same is true of every character, in every play. The characters are continually involved in doing something, in attempting to achieve something—and everything they are doing is related to their "spine." Remember that? We must see everything that the characters do in the light of their "deeper wish." But just as with you and I, the characters actions are sometimes in line with that deeper wish and sometimes not. If not, the character will usually have to pay the price for the results of his misguided actions. (Like the man who was about to get married will have to deal with the results of his affair with the stranger.)

A NOTE: as we continue, we will be working with the Savage monologue. Later, you may go back on your own and use the Tony monologue for further practice.

Now we must get more specific in terms of the character's spine. Out of everything we have done together in our work on the part of Savage, with our deeper insights into what she says and does, we have to come up with a "spine phrase" or "spine statement." This phrase must be a kind of **bottom line** of her own "deeper wish." It must be **pointed outward towards the world** and **global** in its nature. It must also be stated in an **active** way and **it must never be approached from a negative perspective.** (No matter what any character is invoved in, they do not perceive their own actions to be evil or abhorrent. From their point of view, they always have good and justifiable cause to do what they are doing.) Finally, the words you choose for the spine phrase must not be just any words that seem to fit, **the words you choose must be provocative to you personally.** To be clearer, here's an example: You are playing the part of Murk and you decide that his spine is,

"To get my pay for the drink"

Using what I just told you about creating a spine phrase, answer this question now: **why is this not a good spine statement?**

_____

_____

_____

_____

_____

_____

_____

_____

Here's another attempt for Murk,

"To be mean to the people in my bar"

Why is this not a good spine phrase?

_____

_____

_____

_____

_____

_____

_____

_____

Let's look together at the first choice for Murk, "To get my pay for the drink." Here's why I would say that this is not a good spine statement:

1. It is not really the "bottom line" related to Murk's deeper wish. I'll tell you something, money never is. Whenever someone uses money, my next question is, *"Well, what do you want the money for?"* You might answer, *"So Murk can pay the bills and keep running his bar."* And I say, *"Oh yeah? Well, why does he want to run this bar?"* You answer, *"So he can keep April drunk."* And I ask, *"Well why would he want to do that?"* and so on. We have to keep asking these questions until we arrive at what is the driving force underneath everything Murk says and does.

2. "To get my pay for the drink" isn't pointed outwards toward the world, it is self directed. It is also not global in its

scope. By "pointed outwards" I mean that the spine must be stated in such a way that it is open to include others in the world of the character. And when I use the term "global," I mean that it has to include the world of people the character deals with in the play as well as those who are not in the play. It also means that the phrase must encompass all of the things Murk does, not any one thing. So if Murks spine was "To get my pay for the drink," how would that include the relationship Murk has with the beer salesman or the jukebox repairman? It wouldn't. And it must. How would it include his putting on the Santa costume for April? It wouldn't. And it must.

When we look at the second choice, "To be mean to the people in my bar," we see another bad choice. Why?

1. The main thing I wanted to highlight with this example is that the spine phrase must never be stated in the negative. As I said, no character thinks of the things they do negatively. Murk treats Savage and the others the way he does for his own good reasons. The same with keeping April drunk and watering the dead plants.

2. Again, this spine is too limited and confined.

So what might a good spine statement for Murk be? Well, here's a sample—

"To keep all in harmony"

You can see with a statement like this, "to keep all in harmony," we have crafted a phrase that is pointed outwards and at the same time is open enough to include Murk and his own inner sense of equilibrium, the way he runs his bar, his relationship with April, his relationship with all the people who come into his bar as well as with anyone we can imagine he deals with in the rest of his life. Also, the words I chose are active, they ignite an impulse in me to do something! And, the words I chose are provocative to me in a deep way. I can connect with what it would mean to need to control others so that there is harmony in my environment. I can fantasize about what kinds of circumstances would result in me needing so badly to maintain the harmony around me that I would keep the woman who is closest to me in that *"special haze"* and have an unbreakable set of rules that everyone who deals with me must follow. I enjoy imagining having to control my environment for this specific reason; **for this positive reason**—harmony is a good thing, isn't it? One more thing—as I said, the words of this phrase "to keep all in harmony" do something to **me**, they may not be so great for you. If not, this wouldn't be a good spine statement for you. The words you choose must always get your own juices flowing or you've got nothing to work from.

I want you to give this a try now:

Read the play at least one more time through with one question in mind, "What is Savage's spine?" Then look at everything you have written so far for Savage and, when you have an idea, write down a spine phrase for Savage right here:

O   O   O

Let's move into "Doings." (If you prefer, you may call them "actions" or "objectives." As my Grandpa Jack used to say, *"Same difference."* I like to use the term "doings." Somehow, the word just strikes me as less technical.) To do this, we are going to use the Savage monologue. So, here again is the monologue:

1. I don't care. I don't care how you think about me. What d'you want? You want me to act like somebody on TV? This one got this one way an that's how they are? I don't know how I am, who I am. I don't know what I believe. I don't know where to go to find out. I don't know what to do to be the one person that somewhere inside I wanna be. I don't know nothin but the one thing: I gotta move. And you, too. This whole world I'm in's gotta break up an move.

2. We're on the cliff. We were born here. Well, do you wanna die on the cliff? Do you wanna die in bed? Do you think you're gonna live forever? They told us if you jump off the cliff, you die. And you probably do, but fuck it. Fuck it. We don't know that. You don't know nothin you ain't done, an nobody can tell you nothin. Ain't you tired a livin if this is all livin is? And you know it's not. I may be an asshole and I may not know what to do, but you hear what I'm sayin to you, dammit you do. In your heart you do. This is not life. This is not life. This is not life. Ugly women, right Tony? Somethin else. I don't care what.

3. God, gimme somethin else cause this is definitely not it. New eyes new ears new hands. Gimme back my soul from where you took it, gimme back my friends, gimme back my priests an my father, and take this goddamn virginity from off my life. HUNGER HUNGER HUNGER. If somebody don't gimme somethin, I'm gonna die.

4. I wanna play pool. Somebody play pool with me. I come in here a lotta nights, a lotta nights, an I play pool by myself. I like the game. You hit the white ball, and that ball hits another, and it goes somewhere. When I first started, I didn't mind playin alone. But you get tired of it. The balls don't do nothin unless you make 'em do it. It's all you. They're just like stones. It's like I'm some woman lives inna cave and plays with stones. Somebody

play pool with me. You be the cue ball. Hit me and I'll fly. You don't wanna jump yourself, push me off. You can't keep up your courage alone, playin with stones.

As you see, I broke the Savage monologue down into four sections, or "beats." If you've studied acting for any length of time, you've heard that term before. Very simply, a beat is a unit of action. This means that each time there is a change in what the character is doing, there is a new beat. Breaking the script down into beats helps us get very specific in what we are doing throughout the monologue, and of course, throughout the play. As I have said, specificity is always the key. You see the actor must always be a little smarter than the character. For instance, if you were able to ask Murk, "Are you aware that you are so strict about your 'rules' because ultimately, you want to make harmony in your life?" Murk would probably tell you *"What the hell are you talking about? Rules are rules."* But the actor must be more aware; the actor must be able to answer the question "What am I doing specifically right now?" in every moment of the play. Also, you and I may differ in the exact placement of the beats. Thats fine. The ultimate test will come in the actual trying it out with our acting partners. At that point, we may find that the beat changes on a different line than we first thought, that one beat is actually two, or that what we thought was a new beat is actually the character pursuing the same objective in a different manner. (That's called an **adjustment**. I'll be talking more about adjustments soon.)

Let's go back to Savage, but before we examine the beats, we need to come up with a spine phrase; we need to have that guiding spirit behind everything Savage is doing. Here's one I came up with, try it on for size:

"To break through to life."

Now, how did I come up with that? One of the strongest things I experience as I imagine the life of Savage, is the day-in and day-out deadness she feels:

from taking care of her mother *"I looked at her one day and she looked like a dead plant,"*

to being a virgin at thirty-two *"It's like holdin your breath, only you never have to let go."*

From her fear of moving this way or that *"I'm scared of every-thing. I see what could go wrong with everything so I don't do noth-in. I got this one thing in me that I hate. I'm a coward,"*

to her horrendous sense of isolation *"I ain't never been friends with nobody. I ain't had the time. I got my mother. I got the job. I just talk at people, which is lonely. I honestly could just fall down from loneliness."*

Of course, I arrived at the spine not just from her words, I am equally moved by her relationship with Murk and trying to get past "the thing" with him, her struggle to win Tony and take him to a "room with no bed," and her offer to have April move into a new apartment with her and Linda.

Personally, I think she lives in a constant state of bewilder-ment, especially when it comes to the concept of love *"You're a little girl and you see the movies and maybe you talk to your moth-er and you definitely talk to your friends and then you know, right? So you go ahead and you do love. And somethin a what somebody told ya inna movie or in your ear is what love is. And where the fuck are you then, that's what I wanna know? Where the fuck are you when you've done love, and you can point to love, and you can name it, and love is the same as gravity the same as everything else, and everything else is a totally dead fuckin issue?"*

And along with her inner confusion, is an urgent craving to take action *"You can't just keep fillin 'em up an we empty 'em and the night goes by and it's the next day and it's the same thing. That's death. That's death. We gotta get past the thing. We gotta break the sameness."*

But maybe the most powerful image is when Savage talks about her dream and her beautiful eyes that were always there and in these words to Tony: *"I'm tryin to pull off my face so you can see my eyes. Do you wanna see my eyes?"* Who knows why, but that question "Do you wanna see my eyes?" has a big impact on me. My God, I just flashed back on a girlfriend from high school named Marilyn. I'm actually shaking inside right now because I think that's exactly what she was asking me underneath all of her words and behavior. "Do you wanna see my eyes?" I wish I was able to understand it back then.

The ways in which I connect with Savage's vision of what having a "life" might really mean, starts to add up to my first attempt at a spine phrase, "to break through to life." That phrase is open enough and provocative enough to my imagination that it might just work for me. But you know what? I might discover, after getting into "the doings" and rehearsing the monologue, that it doesn't work so well. (And by not working well, I mean that it doesn't inject me into taking action through Savage's point of view.) If it's not as effective as I thought it would be, I would go back and re-work the phrase.

ATTENTION PLEASE! One important note. We don't act the spine. Do you hear that? We cannot act the spine directly. The spine is what makes all the things we will be doing on stage essential. (And this brings us right back to "the doings.")

As we begin to look at the beats and at what we are doing, the first thing we must know is what immediately preceded the monologue—**what and who** is this speech in response to? If we go back to the play, we know that all of Savage's attempts to "break through to life" tonight are failing and it is also becoming clear to her that she's not going to get Tony for herself. So the monologue certainly springs out of her increasingly desperate need not to sink back into the quicksand of her life. We also know that what kicks her off into this speech, in a literal sense, is this exchange:

> LINDA: You know, you're crazy. You're all over the place.
> SAVAGE: You think so?
> LINDA: Yeah, I do. I come in here cryin, you tell me we should be friends an getta apartment. And April too. Then my boyfriend comes in and you start hittin on him, and forget me, right? Now you tell April she should go crazy. Which is a bad idea. How am I supposed to think about you, Denise?"
> SAVAGE: I don't care. I don't care how you think about me. What d'you want? You want me to act like somebody on TV?…

So, on to the doings. Let's try to be as simple as possible about all of this. The first thing we must look for in each beat is what the character is **actually doing**. We may not end up working with the beats in this form, but it is our first step into what's going on. To do this, listen to what Savage is saying and see if you can describe, in each beat, what it is she is doing—in a literal sense—with the others in the bar. For example, in beat one, Savage is reacting to Linda's criticisms. In the way Savage responds to Linda in beat one, it's as if she is saying, "I've got good reasons for doing the things I've done here tonight." We could say that what Savage is actually doing is **"explaining her-**

self to Linda." You might find something else that Savage is doing in beat one or you might agree with me but have another way of saying it. Give this a try now:

*Examine the four beats and write down what you think Savage is **actually doing** in each of the beats. Also, with each doing you find, jot down a few notes as to why you believe that's what she is actually involved in doing. Please write your responses below.*

In beat one, Savage is:
Notes:

_____

_____

_____

_____

In beat two, Savage is:
Notes:

_____

_____

_____

_____

In beat three, Savage is:
Notes:

_____

_____

_____

_____

In beat four Savage is:
Notes:

_____

_____

_____

_____

I already gave you my thoughts for the first beat. Here is what I came up with for the "actual doings" in the other beats:

Beat two—**Opening their eyes**
Beat three—**Pleading with God**
Beat four—**Finding a pool partner**

Did you come up with anything similar? Go back to the beats and see how the doings I found are related to the script. Do they make sense to you?

○　○　○

So, how do we use these doings to help us act the part?

> *"The shortest answer is doing"*
> An English Proverb

> *"An ounce of action is worth a ton of theory"*
> Friedrich Engels

Clearly, the true test of everything we have been talking about up until now, is in the doing of it. We can think about it all we want, but until we actually try to do it, we've got nothing more than an interesting concept. And that's not acting! And, having said that, there are some other things we need to discuss before you get to work with your partner.

This brings up a new question for us: how do we rehearse the monologue? Remember, monologues like the ones we have been examining from *Savage In Limbo*, are actually scenes. Most monologues done for auditions really are scenes in that they involve another person or people that you are talking to. So, with these monologues, I suggest that you rehearse them as you would rehearse a scene—with an acting partner. I don't think it's just helpful to have someone that you can actually talk to when you are working on the piece, I believe it is important.

Consider this:

Imagine a close friend is emotionally devastated because of something awful that has just happened in her life. You love your friend and you want to comfort her.
*What is it, do you think, that will determine **the ways** in which you actually comfort your friend? Write down your thoughts here:*

_____

_____

_____

_____

_____

_____

○ ○ ○

The answer is really a combination of two things that must be in a continual dance with each other—

1: your need and desire
2: what is being communicated to you from the other person.

In other words, the ways in which you go about comforting your friend are an outcome of your true desire to comfort her in relation to what you are getting **from her.** For example: Suppose your friend is crying, so you go over and start to rub her back. But she pushes your arm off of her with a *"Don't!"* and she walks away. Well, you're probably not going to run right over and start rubbing her back again. You'll probably find another way to comfort her. Maybe you'll stand right where you are and say very softly, *"I'm really sorry you're in such pain."* If she then turns to you and reaches out with both arms and says, *"Help,"* you might run over to her and hold her in your arms. And if she suddenly breaks from your arms and runs to her car and drives off, you might call her answering machine and leave a message, *"Listen, I just want you to know that I love you and if you need to talk or if you need anything, please call me. I'll be at work tomorrow from 8:00 AM until noon and if you want to, you can call me there or at home in the afternoon. Try to get some sleep tonight. If I don't here from you, I'll check in with you tomorrow night. Goodnight."* In this particular "beat" of this two-person play, *A Person and An Upset Friend,* you ("the person") have a singular doing, "To comfort a friend." But the way in which you do it changes because of what she ("an upset friend") is communicating to you in each moment. You are **"adjusting"** how you comfort her, as you **"work off"** the meaning of her behavior.

I told you I would come back to it and there it is—**adjustments.** Doings or actions are **what you are doing** and adjustments are **how you do what you are doing.** And who are you continually adjusting to? Your partners on stage! Although you will be performing the monologue alone, as we established, the monologue is really a scene. This means that even though the other person or people are not there, you must be in response to, **working off**, the other character or characters as if they were there. And, you must be adjusting to what they give you. Now it should make more sense when I say that it is important to rehearse the monologue with an acting partner. Working with a partner can help lead you to many discoveries: "Is this the best doing for this beat?" "Did I say it in a way that truly incites me to action?" "Is this really a new beat or is it really an adjustment?" Working with a partner will also help you get out of your head and lead you to surprising ways of going after what you want—ways that you couldn't have come up with on your own. And hey, why not work with someone you enjoy working with? You're going to be doing a bunch of expressing yourself and I think it's a great idea to have someone there with whom you feel safe in going wherever the work takes you.

As we talked about with the spine, the words you choose for the doing must be provocative for you. If they are not, you must keep working on the way you say the doing until the phrase does something to you inside. You will also find that sometimes the thing you determined the character is actually doing is enough to work with—or—many times, you must cut a little deeper. What I mean is this: you must ask yourself if the "actual doing" is really the bottom line or is there a more primary "core" of that doing. For example: if my actual doing was, "cleaning up the guest room," the core of that doing might be, "To make my guest feel welcome." We could call this going from the "actual doing" to the "core doing." Some acting teachers call this shift going from the "literal action" to the "essential action." But you know, we could call it "Marvin!" We don't have to call it anything—what we have to do is find what works, what propels us into fighting to accomplish something and what leads us into viewing the world through "the eyes" of the character.

There are some other things that are helpful when you put together a doing. First, it's very useful to utilize **active verbs**. For example: **to beseech, to scold, to caution, to intimidate, to advise, to correct, to condemn, to praise, to mend, etc**. Using active verbs assist you in being more specific in what you are doing and they also point you towards the other person. The way you say the doing must involve you with the other people you are acting with, it must not be self directed. And so, the following kinds of doings **are not** going to help you: to get excited, to be furious, to be jealous, to be shy, to be in love, etc…These kinds of phrases not only leave out your acting partners, they are general and they require that you be in some generic emotional state. You can not act a generic emotional state! And your attention must never be on emotion anyway, your attention must be where? YES, YES, YES! ON WHAT YOU ARE DOING! Finally, the doing must be something that you can relate to, that you can do—when it is, no matter what the personal demands are, you have a shot at having some fun doing it.

O   O   O

Let's go back to the four beats and talk more specifically about the doings and how to get to work on them. Also, I want to let you know now that you will soon need a partner to work with. So be ready to invite a friend over to do some exploring. Remember, the ultimate learning about doings is out of the experience of doing them. Also, for our purposes right now, please go along with the way I have worded the doings. You can then come back and try out your own doings later.

○ ○ ○

Beat 1

I think that in these circumstances and out of how Linda has just attacked her, Savage is "explaining herself" (that was our actual doing) in order to defend or to take a stand on what she has done, how she feels and who she is. So we move from the actual doing, "to explain," to the more core issue, "to take a stand." Do you see how "to take a stand" is also a stronger and more specific choice? It is certainly more vivid and provocative! So let's work with this as the doing in beat one:

"To take a stand"

Now, to work on the doing, we must go away from the circumstances of the play. (Hang in here with me, this may be a little confusing for a while—but it will get clear.) I am telling you that, we can not act Savage's story and her own need to take a stand. So the next phase of working on the doing is to begin making it our own. Just as we have addressed making what Savage says our own, we must also work on making what she is doing our own. To do this we must ask ourselves, "Under what circumstances would I be compelled **to take a stand?**" We must ask, "What is this thing Savage is doing like for me?" We must answer that question with, "It is **AS IF** _____," and we must fill in that blank with a situation that makes us want and need to do that doing.

Where do we go to for the situation that will fill in the blank? How do we begin to create the circumstances that will inject us into that doing? The answer is, we go to two places in ourselves that must work in unison—1) **our life** and 2) **our imagination.** We go to our life which feeds us that which has true meaning to us, and we go to our imagination which offers an infinite variety of human possibilities. And so, we use an "element of truth" from our life as the heart of the "imaginary circumstances" we shape to take us into the land of the particular doing we are working on—in this case, "to take a stand!" (Remember, acting is living truthfully under imaginary circumstances.)

I want to get clearer. Here's an example of an imaginary situation based on an element of truth that I might use:

Suppose, due to some tragic (and specific) events, I was left homeless, unemployed, without a penny to my name and without any family except for my two children. And because of this, my children were taken from me by a social service agency. Today, I have to appear before a three-person board who will decide if I can have my children back. The meeting begins and one person from the board stands up and says, "You are unstable in every way, you can't provide a safe environment for your children, you can't afford to clothe or to feed them, you have no real and tangible skills that we can see and you are out of your mind if you think there is any way you will persuade us that you should have them back. Face it Mr. Silverberg, you are not getting your kids back!"

What are the imaginary circumstances in that example? All of it is imaginary except for one thing—I do, in fact, have two children and if something like this were to happen, THERE IS NO WAY THAT I WOULD ALLOW ANYBODY TO TAKE MY KIDS AWAY FROM ME—I DON'T CARE WHO THE HELL IT WAS, WHAT THEY THOUGHT WOULD BE BEST OR WHAT ACTIONS I WOULD HAVE TO TAKE TO GET MY CHILDREN BACK!

The element of truth here is my relationship with my children. That is something I really know—I don't have to think about it. My feelings for my children live in me; in my guts, in my mind and in my heart. Wherever the hell things live in us, that's where my children are. Now, around that element of truth, I constructed some imaginary circumstances that make the stakes very high. Well, aren't the stakes high for Savage? You bet your tush they are! She's fighting for her life! So, somehow, I have to get myself into the domain of "to take a stand" because I am fighting for my life. In these circumstances "my life" is everything that being with my children means to me. I have to "take a stand" RIGHT NOW because it means THAT MUCH! I'll say that again. I constructed the imaginary circumstances to compel me to take action **right now**—not next Tuesday, not tomorrow and not in ten minutes. I have to take a stand right now because I can't afford to wait. And the slimeball, low-life, know-nothing social worker who just threatened me isn't going to stand in my way!

Now to work. Here is step one: after coming up with these circumstances, I would give my acting partner this line, "You can't have your kids back, Mr Silverberg!" and I would tell him to say that line to me when we begin and whenever I hesitate as we are working. So **who am I talking to** in this improvisation we will be doing together? I am talking to that slimeball social worker who's committed to destroying my life and my children's lives. Then I would begin talking to him with one intention, "to take a stand" and get my children back! And what fuels that intention? My true desire to have my children back. Do I sit and figure out what to say before I start talking? NO, I JUST START TALKING. Do I sit and figure out how to "take a stand" before I start working? NO, I JUST START WITH THE INTENTION TO "TAKE A STAND" AND I WILL DISCOVER HOW TO DO IT AS I DO IT. Do you get that?

It's crucial! You will stumble upon and uncover how to "take a stand" in the real attempt to do it and as you are in real contact with your acting partner. Also, it is helpful every once in a while to say your doing out loud as you are talking to your partner. That might sound like this:

My Partner: *You can't have your kids back, Mr Silverberg.*

Me: *Listen you piece of dirt, there is no way in hell you are going to keep my kids from me. I am their father and no matter what you think of me and how little money I have, I will take care of them. I AM TAKING A STAND and you better sit down and listen before I make you sit down—those are my kids and no one knows what they need like I do—stay out of my way unless you want more trouble than you know how to deal with. I may not have my life together like you think I should or have all the perfect elements that make up the ideal TV family, but I've got everything my children need for a good life…*

As I talk, I am free associating (as we have done in the writing exercises) in a way that is shaped by the meaning of the circumstances I created and by the doing I have given myself. This is what you will be doing with your partner. And by saying the doing out loud every so often, you keep in aim of what you are trying to accomplish. After a while, as the doing "takes root" you don't need to say the action anymore because you're DOING IT. This "taking root" is good to point out right here. Please don't expect to start talking to your partner and, BINGO, you are fully doing the action. Once your partner says the words you gave him or her to say to you, jump in and go after what you are fighting for:

- Just keep talking, don't stop.
- Try not to pause—just keep going, keep going.

- When you don't have the words, talk anyway.
- Say whatever comes out of your mouth.
- Try not to censor anything.
- Keep throwing that doing in there. Say it out loud.

If the circumstances that you set up really mean something to you, and the doing is a strong one, there is a good chance that you and the doing will start to come together; the doing and the meaning behind why you are doing it, will "take root" in you and you will shift into a place of living the action in ways that will surprise you. But to get there, you must give yourself the permission to go through the uncomfortable period where you feel like you don't know what you are doing and you want to quit. If you keep going when the urge to quit is strongest, if you keep talking when you don't have the words and if you keep "taking a stand" when you don't know how to do it—you may unearth some beautiful life!

Okay, it's your turn. Complete the following first:

*I want you to spend some time and come up with **imaginary circumstances** based on **an element of truth**. In these circumstances, the stakes must be high and they must propel you into the strong need to "take a stand." On the following blank page, write down the circumstances that you will be working with and who you are talking to—you must know who you are "taking a stand" with. Also, write down a line to give to your acting partner that he or she will say to you as the two of you work together.*

Circumstances _____

_____

_____

_____

_____

_____

_____

_____

_____

_____

_____

_____

_____

_____

I'm talking to _____

_____

_____

_____

Line for my partner _____

_____

_____

_____

_____

Did you come up with something? Finding just the right circumstances to work with is certainly challenging. As you work, you may find that the circumstances work for you or that they don't really take you into the doing in the way you had hoped. In that case, you have to go back and either re-work the way you set up the circumstances or find new ones. So, if you have come up with something to work with, let's move on.

I now want you to give your partner the words you came up with for her or him. Make sure your partner knows that they will say this "line" to begin your work together. **Also tell him or her to say the line to you whenever you seem to get stuck or pause or start thinking about what to do next.** Before you start, look at your partner and in your mind, take just a moment to remind yourself of what's happening (the imaginary circumstances) so that you know who you are talking to and exactly why you must "take a stand" right now. Then nod to your partner, letting her know she may begin. Your partner will say the line to you and you will leap, immediately, into "taking a stand." As I said before, don't worry about **how** to "take a stand," **you will discover how—as you do it.** Why is this important? Because there is a part of you that knows how to do it in better ways than you could ever come up with in your head. And remember, once you start talking:

- Just keep talking, don't stop.
- Try not to pause—just keep going, keep going.
- When you don't have the words, talk anyway.
- Say whatever comes out of your mouth.
- Try not to censor anything.
- Keep throwing that doing in there. Say it out loud.
- TAKE A STAND!

Are you ready? I can't really tell you how long to work for. Experiment. See if the doing begins to click inside. Give it a few good attempts. If, ultimately, the circumstances don't seem to take you very far, go back and re-work them or create new ones.

Please work with your partner now and when you feel like you have started to really connect with the doing, come back to the book.

○   ○   ○

Now that you have taken a step into the land of "taking a stand," I want you to learn the words of beat one. Learn them as if they were one long sentence. It even helps if you write them on a piece of paper that way—like one sentence without any punctuation. So, go ahead and write the words down in that manner and then learn them so you know them inside and out. What I mean is, learn them so well that you could spit those words out no matter what else was happening around you. Here again are the words from beat one. Take whatever time you need to learn them before you move on to the next assignment. (You will notice that I wrote the beat with no punctuation.)

I don't care I don't care how you think about me what d'you want you want me to act like somebody on TV this one got this one way an that's how they are I don't know how I am who I am I don't know what I believe I don't know where to go to find out I don't know what to do to be the one person that somewhere inside I wanna be I don't know nothin but the one thing I gotta move and you too this whole world I'm in's gotta break up an move

○   ○   ○

Now that you have learned the words, we will continue. Once again you will need your partner to work with. So get your partner and go on to the next step.

○   ○   ○

You are now going to start by doing exactly what you did with your partner last time. (Don't try to repeat word for word what you did last time, simply remind yourself of your imaginary circumstances and then get into "taking a stand." Leave the words alone, they will be freely supplied.)

There is one addition to the exercise. When you feel like you are really starting to get into the doing, "To take a stand," I want you to switch from speaking out of your own circumstances and go into the words of the script. In other words, as you sink into the reality of your own imaginary circumstances, and the meaning of "taking a stand" deepens, I want you to jump to the words of beat one and speak those words. Do not stop anything that is going on for you. Do not change the way you are talking in that moment. Simply go from your own words to the words of beat one as if it was all just one speech. When you switch to the words from the script, say a few lines and then go back to your own circumstances. Continue to "take a stand" and when you've got that going, go back to the script again. When you go back to the script, begin again from the first line of beat one, but this time go an extra line or two. Work in this manner, going back and forth from your own words to the words of the script until you have done the whole beat. What you will experience as you work in this way, is that the words from the script will "ride on" the meaning that is living in you—the meaning brought to life from the work you have done on your imaginary circumstances and your own personal need to "take a stand."

Here is what this exercise might sound like if I were doing it with my own imaginary circumstances that I gave you as an example earlier (the lines from Savage's speech are in bold):

You sit down and listen to me. There is no way you are going to keep my kids. I will make your life miserable if you try to get in my way. No matter what you say or do those kids are mine and **I don't care. I don't care how you think about me. What d'you want? You want me to act like somebody on TV? This one got this one way an that's how they are?** *Those kids are coming home with me today and not one of you can stop me. Those kids belong with me, I am a good father and I have always been a good father and I'll get back on my feet here real soon and* **I don't care. I don't care how you think about me. What d'you want? You want me to act like somebody on TV? This one got this one way an that's how they are?** **I don't know how I am, who I am. I don't know what I believe. I don't know where to go to find out.** *But I know that those kids are mine and they will be with me no matter what you say or do...* (and so on until I get through the whole beat.)

Now I want you to give it a try with your partner. When you have done this step, come back and read on.

O   O   O

By the way, this work we are doing is quite demanding. To grab a hold of it, it takes alot of consistent practice. So, please be patient with yourself. And keep working the exercise.

O   O   O

After you have gotten a grasp of the last exercise with your partner, I want you to do two more things.

1. Begin with your partner in the same way you have—think of your imaginary circumstances for a moment, have your partner say the words you supplied to him or her and then you "take a stand" and speak from your own circumstances. This time, when you get it going, switch to the words of the script and **do the entire first beat**. Do this a few times, each time exploring the doing as you work with your partner.

○ ○ ○

2. After completing exercise number one from above, I want you to begin by thinking of your imaginary circumstances for a moment and then without any words from your partner, begin speaking to your partner using only the words from the script. Is that clear? You will now only use the words from the script as you fight to "take a stand." Do the entire first beat. Do this a few times.

○ ○ ○

We have been working on bringing a personal life and a reality of doing to the words from the script. Now you better understand something I mentioned earlier in the book. That when you perform the piece, the audience is getting two things at one time—on a conscious level, they get the story of the words, but on a gut level, they are impacted by the personal life you have brought to the words. They are moved by witnessing and experiencing you truly trying to accomplish something because it **actually** means that much to you.

There is something else I hope you are beginning to discover out of this approach; something most actors never understand because they are trying to "act the words." What I'm talking about is that the words we speak don't always reflect what it is we are really doing. But most actors try to illustrate the words because they don't really know what they are doing or why. For example, just because Savage says *"I don't know how I am, who I am. I don't know what I believe. I don't know where to go to find out. I don't know what to do to be the one person that somewhere inside I wanna be,"* it doesn't mean that she's giving up on life. No! She's taking a stand on life! ***"THIS WHOLE WORLD I'M IN'S GOTTA BREAK UP AND MOVE!"*** But the trap that most actors will fall into is illustrating those "I don't know…" lines as if she was giving up because they want to match the words with the action. Illustrating the words always leads you to the clichés of acting.

Once you get the hang of it, this is a wonderful approach to personalizing the doings. What I suggest now is that together, we complete talking about the doings for the rest of the beats. Then, if you are a woman, I'd like you to continue to work on this monologue with your partner as we have just been doing and see how far you can take it. If you want some more practice, you men might enjoy going back to the Tony speech and working on all of these steps to bring that monologue to life. Either way, let's all continue to look at the doings for beats two, three and four and how you then put the whole piece together.

Beat 2

We said that what Savage was actually doing was "opening their eyes." I happen to like this doing and want to use it to work with. I don't think we need to change it in any way. So work on the doing:

"To open their eyes"

Important Note: The only other thing I want you to know as you prepare to work on beat two and the other beats, is that you don't have to come up with a whole new set of imaginary circumstances for each beat. I think it is most effective for working on a monologue to continue using the same circumstances with this new guiding light, *"To open their eyes."* And you will work this way with all of the beats for the monologue—incorporating the imaginary circumstances that you created with the specific intention of the doing you have determined for each beat. So, in my example circumstances, I would be talking to the social workers who have my children and I would now be "opening their eyes!"

To make this clear for you, let me give you an example of what the free association might sound like in this beat. Again, I will be using my same imaginary circumstances, but this time, I will be guided by the doing for beat two, "To open their eyes."

You have to realize what a huge mistake you're making here. Can't you see how you are about to destroy the lives of people who are already hurting. OPEN YOUR EYES, these are two little children who need their father and you are going to devastate them in ways that will damage them for life. You have to see that you are making a big mistake, there is no good reason to take this action. Look at me, damn it, really look at me, OPEN YOUR EYES, you've got to see that I care more about those two kids than anybody in the world....(etc.)

Beat 3

We said that the actual doing was "Pleading with God." I think that Savage is pleading so that she can receive a solution. I think that the core of the doing in this beat is:

"To demand a solution"

Beat 4

We said that the actual doing was "finding a pool partner."
Here, it's obvious that it is much more than a pool partner that
Savage is after. I think what she really wants is a friend. Don't
you think Savage would just love to have a real friend? So why
don't we try that as a doing:

"To make a friend"

o   o   o

Putting the monologue together now is the logical next step
after you have done all the work on the beats. When you have
fully worked the beats, the meaning you have brought to the
words will live in you and you will not have to think about the
doings anymore. Just like tying your shoes, once you have
worked and worked and worked all the steps, you do it auto-
matically. Well, after you have worked the beats, you will be
injected into the doings simply by speaking the words of the
monologue.

So when you have fully worked the beats, work with your
partner and try putting beat one and two together as one speech.
(Always begin your work by reminding yourself of your own
imaginary circumstances.) Then go back and do beats one, two
and three as one speech. Finally, do all four beats. Anytime you
feel like you are losing touch with what you are doing, simply
say the doing of that beat outloud to your partner and continue
with the monologue. After working this way, continue by working the whole monologue each time.

Now you have got the basis of a monologue and a way to
explore material. Each time you do the monologue it should be

an improvisation in that you must always feel free to express yourself out of what is actually happening for you in the moment. If you try to make any rehearsal or performance be what it was the last time, it's dead. Risk going where each rehearsal takes you as you continue to do the monologue with your partner. Of course, in the audition, your partner won't be there. The next step then is to rehearse without your partner. If you have made the foundation very strong in your work with your partner, you will see that you can do the piece and retain all of the meaning, the doings and the adjustments that you have discovered **as well as discovering new ones**—without your partner present.

What about blocking? You have noticed I haven't said a word about it. I'll tell you, when I was studying acting, one of my teachers at the Playhouse, Phil Gushee, told us something I have always remembered. Phil said that the best audition he had ever seen was one in which the person was so absolutely authentic and so filled with life that Phil was mesmerized. He also told us that the guy auditioning sat in a chair very close to him throughout the audition, and never raised his voice above a whisper. Now, I'm not telling you to sit in a chair and whisper. I am telling you that fancy blocking isn't going to do a damn thing for the monologue. Yet most actors come in with these carefully laid out moves for the monologue—sit on this line, leap up at this moment, raise the hands to the sky here, fall to the ground there—and you know what? The difference between an actor doing preconceived blocking in the attempt to be interesting and the actor who really knows what they are saying and doing and **moves out of the true need to move**, is very very clear. The simple answer is, don't do anything unless something in you has to do it. **If there is no true impulse to move, don't move. If you do have the impulse to move or to leap or to punch the air or whatever—DO IT AND DO IT AT 100**

PERCENT! The point of Phil's example to us was that it is not the blocking that will make the piece interesting. If you are worried about being boring without a bunch of moving around, then you haven't done your homework. Give yourself the permission to be still, to start from stillness and find out where you have to move and if you have to move. And feel free to discover this each time you perform the piece. You may surprise yourself and surprise the people watching—wouldn't that be great!

One more thing. On the day of your audition, please don't sit around doing your monologue a thousand times. By this day, you should be absolutely prepared and ready to perform the monologue. So spend your time in creative and fun ways. Certainly do a great warm-up and stretch; really get into your body. Go over the monologue one time. But don't really act it, just sit quietly and go over your imaginary circumstances and say the words very simply one time. Then go out into the world and spend some time living through "the eyes" of the thing you are trying to accomplish in the imaginary circumstances you have been working with.

For instance, if I was using the circumstances about my children being taken away, I might leave early for the audition and go into a drug store. In the store, I might buy a greeting card that I would want to give to my children. When I got to the audition, rather than going over and over my monologue, or talking with other actors, I would sit by myself and write to my children on that card, telling them how much I loved them and for them not to worry—that they would be back with me very soon. Every time I looked up at the entrance into the room where the auditions were being held, I would see the entrance to the meeting room with the social workers. The other actors around me would all be other people who were waiting to go into their own meetings with the social workers. I would look at their faces and ask myself, "What kind of desperate situation are they in?" When I was called to go in and audition, I would say something to myself like "I'm getting my kids back—no matter what!" Then, as I entered the room, I'd drop it all and I would turn myself over to the people in the room. I would greet them and make them feel welcome at my audition. I would treat them the way I would like to be treated at an audition. Then, when they said it was time to work, I would become quiet and still for just a few moments, remind myself that I want my children back and I'd begin the monologue.

○   ○   ○

Section Two

Loving to Audition:
A Living Approach

chapter 4

Identifying Your Attitudes about Auditioning

READ THE FOLLOWING FIRST!

To begin the exploration of your own attitudes toward auditioning, on the next page are a number of unfinished statements. You will be completing each sentence with your own words. Write your first response to each statement as quickly as you can and without pausing, move on to the next statement. Continue in this manner until the entire exercise is finished. Write whatever comes to your mind and try not to censor anything—whether it's one word or fifty, write it down!

Are you ready?

DO NOT GO TO THE REFRIGERATOR!

DO NOT CALL 911!

JUST GO!

1. Auditions are....

_____

_____

_____

_____

2. On the day of my audition I...

_____

_____

_____

_____

3. When I am about to go in to do my audition I...

_____

_____

_____

_____

4. I wish auditions...

_____

_____

_____

_____

5. While I'm auditioning I...

_____

_____

_____

_____

6. Those people holding the auditions are...

_____

_____

_____

_____

7. In "under two minutes" I can show them...

_____

_____

_____

_____

8. Getting the part is...

_____

_____

_____

_____

9. If the auditioners really worked with me, they would know that...

_____

_____

_____

_____

10. When I leave the audition I...

_____

_____

_____

_____

That's it, you're done. Take a deep breath.

O   O   O

Before continuing with the book, go and get a box of colored pencils. Then come back to the book as soon as you can. Go ahead and do that please—do not continue reading. Hey! No more reading, go and find some colors.

O   O   O

Welcome back. Now, I want you to go back and read your responses to the statements. Take your time. After reading your own responses, go to the box below. Using your pencils, draw a picture of how you feel after reading what you wrote in the writing exercise. Don't waste any energy trying to make a pretty, clever or interesting picture—just begin drawing and see if you can allow yourself to discover what emerges as you draw. After you are done, read on.

Now, I want you to re-read the comments you wrote in the writing exercise, take a good look at your drawing and then use this page to write down anything that you have discovered about your own attitudes, thoughts and feelings around this thing called auditioning.

_____

_____

_____

_____

_____

_____

_____

_____

_____

_____

_____

_____

_____

_____

_____

_____

_____

_____

_____

_____

_____

_____

chapter 5

What Gets in the Way
of Enjoying Auditioning

Loving To Audition. What was your first response when you read that title? Most actors I have mentioned it to laugh out loud when they hear it. It's a laugh that says, "If only that were true." The truth is, most actors I know love to get the job, they love to rehearse and they love to perform—but they do not love to audition, they simply put up with it.

Now, imagine being married to a person you don't love, staying with that person your entire life and just "putting up with them." Think about what you might be thinking and feeling as you come home each day, as you approach the door and as you enter your unhappy home. What a discouraging and painful way to live that would be.

As actors, we face a life of auditioning—we are married to it. It is clear to me that, for our own well-being as well as becoming more effective in our auditioning, we must find a way to have fun with the whole crazy thing. To fall in love with it! I'll tell you something, if you're not having fun in your auditions— no one else will either. And listen, the folks holding the auditions want to have some fun when you come in. And what I mean by fun is, they want someone to come in and wake them up, someone who will ignite their interest! They are praying that you are fantastically alive and courageous. Because most of what they have seen before you has definitely not been fantastically alive and courageous. Most of it has been just the opposite.

What is it, do you think, that makes the audition event so dreaded and feared by most actors. Let's bring to light some of the issues contributing to this anxiety.

The Seven Sources of Anxiety:

1. Comparisons
"The other actors auditioning are better than me! They must be…well they certainly look more the part. And there's too many of them—how can there be so many actors auditioning for this one little part, I don't like these odds. And look at how good they are at bullshitting, they are so much more confident and at ease than I am. Their resumes must show more credentials and experience than mine. And look at that great headshot he's got. Mine stinks. And they all seem to know each other and I don't know any of them. I'm such an outsider, how the hell do I break in? Why didn't I dress like them, why don't I look like them, why can't I act like them, be like them, talk like them, smile like them. Why can't I be them!"

2. Preparation
"I wish I spent more time working on this monologue. I'm not really ready to do it, the end of it is still so weak. I wish I got some feedback from someone before doing it for an audition—how the hell do I know if anything's gonna happen today when I do it. Why didn't I work harder, what's wrong with me?" -OR-

"I've done this damn monologue so much I just don't really care about it anymore, oh shit I'll just do it and get it over with. Why the hell should I put something new together just for this stupid audition, my chances are one in a million for this damn part anyway."

3. Talent

"Am I talented, will they think I'm talented, some actors are truly gifted, am I? I think I'm talented and they have to recognize that I am talented, will they? Am I really talented, how talented? What is talent anyway, I want them to see that I do have talent, oh God please let them see my talent."

4. Time

"How the hell can I show them anything in two damn minutes. How stupid! What if they stop me in the middle of my piece, that will really suck, I mean, the end's the best part! If they stop me before I finish I'll scream, I'll demand that they let me finish…I'll curse them out, I'll give them the finger, rip up my damn photo & resume and storm out…I'll just pretend I didn't hear them and I'll finish the monologue…I'll smile and say they just have to hear the best part…I'll ask them to just give me a few more seconds…I'll get on my knees and beg to have just a little more time…"

5. Small Talk

"What should I say when I introduce myself. I have nothing interesting to say. I don't want to talk, I want to do my audition. I shouldn't be judged on how clever or amusing I can be. I hate talking about myself, I just want to get the audition going and do my work. I just don't feel like talking before I do the monologue and after it's over I just want to get the hell out of there. Why don't they just leave me alone!"

6. "I don't know what they want."

"How do I know what they want, why don't thay say what the hell they are looking for so I can give it to them. Maybe they'll say something when I get in there. Damn it, I'll give them whatever they want, I'll be whatever they want, I'll do whatever they want. I may not even be close to what they want. If they would just say what they want, I wouldn't have to waste all my damn time on this audition to begin with. What in the world do they want from me, what?"

7. "They're something—I'm nothing."

"They're in charge, they've got the position, the money, and they will do whatever they please. What do I have? I just want them to like me and give me a part. I want them to like me, please let them like me. Maybe they'll give me the job, they probably won't, but maybe they will. Please let them like me, I want to get this one, I really want it, I have to get this one, I just have to! I'll go nuts if I don't get this one, I'll just die, they have to give it to me, I want it bad. They'll see that in my eyes, I will make them see how much I want this one. They will give it to me, I'll make them give it to me, I'll make them! Oh God, I'm so powerless, I can't make them do a damn thing, they'll do whatever they please. Who am I anyway."

○   ○   ○

Well, did you find yourself reflected in any of those thoughts. With all that garbage running through our heads, how in the world can we enjoy auditioning when what we really wish was that we could abolish the whole, barbaric practice.

Lastly, I did want to note one other facet which is possibly more subtle. A lot of us actors believe that not only are we supposed to walk around life depressed and miserable but that it is in fact, necessary to our art. That living in a continual state of upset is good for our acting instrument. So feeling frustrated, anxious and pissed off about auditioning becomes just one more welcome element in the turbulent waters we're swimming around in. I'll tell you, when I graduated from the Neighborhood Playhouse and hit the streets of NY, I spent a bunch of years playing that number myself. Not only did I think leading a life in turmoil was empowering, in its own twisted fashion, it was comfortable and I was successful in my acting. Also, I felt at home in it. Growing up, my whole family was always upset—I don't remember anyone talking, everyone was always yelling. It actually felt great to have discovered a profession where I could be perpetually distraught and where it was accepted, supported by my peers and made me better at what I do.

I can tell you now, in no uncertain terms, that it's a bunch of crap. Personally, I've discovered that the process and search to become emotionally healthy and to live a balanced, more peaceful life has not only made my life more enjoyable and fruitful, it absolutely has given me a vast and powerful freedom to act, to be creative. And as I just said, it's a process. Am I always balanced and peaceful? NO! Do I sometimes sneak back into the joy of "feeling like shit" routine? YES! (But I have gotten much better at re-surfacing more quickly. I also have a fantastic wife and two very powerful children who give me little space to walk around for long in my tormented attire!) Try to remember, as you go through this workbook, that it's all a process. And isn't that what theatre is all about? It's never about the answer, it's always about the search, the deep need, the brave attempt, the "striving for" against all odds! Also, when you talk with or read about great artists, you find that not one of them believe they have "arrived."

chapter 6

The Ingredients for Finding Pleasure in Auditioning

If we were now to try and simplify the reason auditioning is not a lot of fun for most actors, I think we have to look at where we are focusing; where we are placing our attention. I say, if you take a hard look, it becomes clear that most actors have their attention on the results. In other words, on getting the job. Now, that may seem to make sense, isn't that what auditioning is all about anyway?

Let's back up. You know, having one's attention on the results goes against everything that being an artist is about. And if it is true in terms of the artistic and creative process, then it is true about life itself. Now, I'm not talking about how we mostly live our lives. That's another story. I'm talking about the nature of aliveness. And if we expect to bring some aliveness into that audition room, this is something actors need to know something about. (And that's what I'll be going into in detail in Chapter 7 of this section.)

So, of course we want the job. We are actors and we want to act. *"Well,"* you might say, *"then that has to be the motivating force to get out there and do the audition!"* I say, we have to look deeper. Because, you know what? Getting the job is always out of our control. Always. Unless you produce the show youself. But no matter how good an actor you and I are, the final result—getting or not getting the job—is out of our hands. And for so many reasons. So, my suggestion is that we take our attention away from what we have no control over and put it somewhere else. Why not put our focus and our energy into what we do have control over. It is in this shift of focus that we start to find some true enjoyment and freedom in our auditioning. So what is it that is in our control?

Before I get to that, I want to have you do another writing exercise. So when you are ready, respond to the statement below. Take your time and write everything that you have to say. Do that now.

○   ○   ○

In my heart, I long to act because...

_____

_____

_____

_____

_____

_____

_____

_____

_____

_____

_____

I think it is so easy in the rush of getting through the demands of our daily lives to lose contact with that sacred spark that brought us to acting in the first place; a time when we may have had no real understanding of why, how or when—but just a gut level knowing that we had something we desperately wanted to say, to share, to express through the art form of acting. So, of course we want to get the job and have a chance to fulfill this deep-seated and very personal need. But we have to see that when our attention is focused on getting the job we immediately set up an inner current of fear because we know that we may not get it. And if we are only finding pleasure in getting the job, we're setting ourselves up for some pain because very few of us actors will get the part every time we audition. So what I am suggesting is that we can find satisfaction in our auditioning whether we get the job or not.

What is it that is in our control? In life, the only thing we truly have control over is what we do. How we then feel about it or how other people respond to it, is always out of our control. Yet, most of us waste a great deal of our time trying to control how things turn out. We manipulate our environment and the people around us so that everything will turn out the way we think it should. We begin to do this at a very early age, although it is not how we began.

When we are first born we are completely and fully the expression of who we truly are in every moment; being ourselves without any thought as to how we will be received or how we are going to be judged. We have very specific needs and we let the world know it in the most direct way we can. We don't beat around the bush and we don't wait for the "appropriate" time or place to have our say. We also let others know how they are making us feel without worrying about the ramifications of being too loving towards them or being too upset with them.

As we grow up, we become concerned with our very survival. We want to be liked and we want to be "right" at all costs. This may be looking good in the eyes of our friends or it might be avoiding getting punished by our parents. Steering us in the direction of what we percieve is safe, comfortable and known is the job of the head. And the ways in which we go about manipulating our environment may be subtle or blatant. Of course, others are busy trying to make us think highly of them and getting us to fit into their own specific picture of how things should go. It's good to start to notice the ways in which we and those around us attempt to control circumstances, because it is here we realize that indeed, we truly are all players on the stage of life. And when we know that we each hold within us the possibility of all human behavior, we become less judgmental as we gain in understanding and compassion for both the people in our lives and for the characters whose realities it is our job, as actors, to take on. Also, as we observe the fascinating and infinte variety of ways we and those around us are "acting" in life, we start to see that everything we do is in some specific way purposeful. And the same, of course, is true for every character in every well-written play.

Let me give you a few examples:

When I was five years old, before she got her driving license, my mother would take my little sister and I in a taxi to go shopping at a large department store called Mays. We did this at least once a week for the groceries and whatever else my mom was shopping for. I remember watching the streets very carefully whenever we would go there and I memorized them. I can't remember why I wanted to do it, but I came up with a scheme to take my best friend Stewie on a walking trip to Mays, which was about five miles from our homes in Levittown, N.Y. It was a warm summer morning and I took my sister Debbie, two years old, and we walked over to Stewie's house. He came out with his little brother, also two years old. I enticed them into going on the journey by telling them all about a special store, a magical place where they gave free toys and candy to all kids. I told them that I would take them all there today. I still remember turning the corner holding Debbie's hand, Stewie and his little brother behind us, also holding hands, and the tremendous excitement of taking them on this journey without our mothers knowing about it. We were gone most of the day. My sister remembers getting to the store and waving to Tony, a friend of my parents who worked there and who thought that we were probably shopping with my mom. She also remembers on our walk back home, someone bumping into Stewie's brother who in turn fell on Debbie who fell to the sidewalk and cut her lip. She remembers crying and calling for her mommie. And we both remember our panic when a policeman pulled up and asked me, "Are you Larry Silverberg?" and put the four of us in the police car. I thought I was going straight to prison and when I got home to the reception of hysterical screams and the whacks I got from my mother, I wished prison was where the cop had taken me.

When I was about eight years old, I had a belief that I could take a screw driver and a hammer and fix anything electronic. I actually knew nothing about repairing things, I just liked to take them apart and see all the little parts that made them work. We had now moved to Merrick, which is where I grew up and from third grade until this very day, my friend Dick and I were and are, best buddies. We lived down the street from each other and there wasn't a single day that we weren't together. One day we were up in Dick's room trying to play with his reel-to-reel tape recorder and the thing just wouldn't work. We plugged it into the wall but no matter what we tried with our little tool kit, the reels wouldn't turn. I told Dick if he just let me unscrew the back and open the thing up, I knew exactly how to fix it. But

Dick said no and went out to get his big brother or father to help. I noticed the door was closed and I was sure that in a flash, I could get this thing running. I proceeded to take off the back and I stuck the screw driver into the mesh of electric parts, started jiggling everything I could, when suddenly there was a BOOM! But not just a BOOM, a BOOM accompanied by mushrooming clouds of thick, white smoke which filled the room instantly. This must have been an atomic powered tape recorder! I heard screams and yells from downstairs and I ran to open Dick's window to get the smoke out before anyone caught me. The door slammed open and Dick and his mother came running into the foggy room. I don't remember exactly what Dick's mom yelled, but it was something like, "WHAT'S ALL THIS SMOKE!" I stood there by the window and answered as absolutely calmly and innocently as I could, "What smoke?" Dick's mom ran back out and I told Dick that I never even touched the tape recorder, it just suddenly exploded. Dick was too frantic to argue. He told me that the electricity went off in the whole house and that I nearly killed his Grandmother who was downstairs, in the middle of re-charging the electric pacemaker in her heart. Years later, Dick told me that he never forgot that moment when I said "What smoke?" He told me that when I said it, I was shaking and that I was white as a ghost.

Something else happened back then that, to this day, I feel absolutely horrible and guilty about. I was in fourth grade and I was at school. We were on our lunch break. It was a warm day and so we were outside in the playground. I remember standing on the grass by myself, swinging a baseball bat and over to my left was this one kid who was a really good athlete and the real popular guy in our class. He was goofing around with a whole bunch of his buddies. I was very fat as a child and not one of his group though, of course, I wanted desperately to be included. I wanted desperately for this grade school idol, who was always the captain for every team, to pick me to play on his team too. So I was swinging this bat and I remember that, though I was a righty, I was practicing swinging it as a lefty. There was also a boy in our class who seemed to be even more of an outsider to the "in-crowd" than me. He was a little overweight and kind of messy all the time. But the main thing about him was that he wore extremely thick glasses, and behind those glasses, his eyes were continually and rapidly moving back and forth. I didn't know that he was standing behind me to the right, and when I took this one really big lefty swing, I swung the bat all the way around and hit him really hard on the shoulder. I remember seeing the shock on his face when the bat came into contact with his body. I remember my own shock in hitting him. He grabbed his arm yelling and hopped on one foot in pain as the "cool" guys all started laughing at him. Suddenly, though I felt really bad for hitting him, I was laughing at him also. Laughing, feeling sick inside for hurting him and stepping closer to the the group of the fourth grade elite to laugh along with them and be "one of the gang." Now, I don't remember what the rest of that school day was like but I do remember, so specifically, getting home from school that day. I went straight to my room and closed my door. I laid down on my bed, put my face in my pillow and I wept. I cried and I cried and I wanted so badly to say sorry to that kid for hurting him and for laughing with the others. I didn't go down to dinner that night because I felt so horribly ill and I couldn't stop crying. I don't remember ever saying sorry or saying anything at all to that boy about what happened, but I know that I have wanted to ever since. I still do today.

I thought I'd mention one other thing. As I grew up, I did lose weight. Actually, I went to the other extreme and at one point I stopped eating and became truly emaciated. In my early twenties, I balanced out in terms of eating and weight and this was also when I became a very active member of *The Pathwork*, which had a facility in Phoenicia, in upstate New York, and another center in New York City. *The Pathwork* was a spiritual community and offered psychotherapy that was spiritually centered. It was a wonderful gift to find *The Pathwork* at this point in my life and I went weekly to both private and group therapy sessions. Very early on, in one of my first sessions actually, my therapist asked if I was aware of all the extra energy I put into my eyes. I wasn't aware of it at all. But soon after he asked, I could feel the way I was using my eyes. And as I began to investigate what that was about, I began to understand very clearly that when I was with people, I wanted to keep their attention above my neck so that they wouldn't see the rest of me. Even though I was no longer fat on the outside, I was still Larry, the little fat boy trying to hide what I looked like. With this awareness, my eyes softened and I relaxed my attempts to control how people "looked" at me.

Again, our profitless attempts to control life are all about survival. But you know what, life won't be controlled. It takes so much of our energy to try and make things go the way we want them to go. It also reveals a lack of faith in the natural wisdom and the goodness of the universe. Am I getting too "spiritual" for you right now? Maybe so, but I'll tell you, I believe it is crucial for every actor to become in some way "spiritually" grounded. I'm not advocating any one way and **I'm not talking about religion, I am talking about encouraging one's own deeper listening.** Because when we do tune in and really listen, we find a guidance that is not merely from the head. And where is the connection to our acting? Now listen, let's get this very clear. Do you really think that over here to the left, you are an actor, and over here to the right, you are a human being? You must get that there is no separation, you are one. Hopefully you will not try to be an actor who acts, but a human being who acts. So we are talking about moving away from being led by the head and moving towards being led by our instinctual self, our center of truth. In our lives, our heads get us into a lot of trouble and in our acting our heads always lead to the clichés of performance. As I said earlier, our heads are always moving us to what is already known because that is what is safe and comfortable. But true acting is never about being comfortable; **true acting is always about going towards what is not yet known for that is where the act of creation occurs.**

I want to move into another writing exercise right now. There will be four parts to this one. So, when you are ready, continue on.

○ ○ ○

1. Write about a time when someone tried to make you do something you really didn't want to do, but you did it anyway. Talk about how that person treated you, how you felt inside, why you did what they wanted, what you did or didn't communicate to them and how the whole event played out.

_____

_____

_____

_____

_____

_____

_____

_____

_____

_____

2. Write about a time you really wanted something or wanted to make something happen and you were successful. But sometime later (or in looking back at it now) you realized that it wasn't really very important or even that it was not very good for you in some way and had a negative impact on you and/or others.

_____

_____

_____

_____

_____

_____

_____

_____

_____

_____

_____

_____

_____

_____

_____

_____

_____

_____

_____

_____

_____

3. Write about a time someone did something that upset you very much but you didn't tell them. Talk about why you didn't say anything. What were your fears about speaking up.

_____

_____

_____

_____

_____

_____

_____

_____

_____

_____

_____

_____

_____

_____

_____

_____

_____

_____

_____

_____

_____

4. I want you to take a few minutes to close your eyes and have the following fantasy. Spend as much time as you want in the fantasy and then continue on to the next page for instructions.

> *Imagine waking up and finding that for one day you have no need to control how anything goes. As you go through a day of your life, you discover that all the people you know and deal with have no desire to control you or what you do. As things occur on this day, you do nothing to change the ways things happen, you simply "go with it" and discover where it leads you. You notice that you are expressing to the people in your life, in a very simple and straightforward manner, exactly what you are experiencing; the people in your life are doing the same with you. You also find that the people you talk with really listen to you with no desire to change you—and that you are listening to them with no need or desire to have them be any different than they are.*

Write about your fantasy. What was the day like? What was being with other people like? Did you notice anything about your energy, the way you walked, your attitude? What were some things you discovered in this fantasy?

_____

_____

_____

_____

_____

_____

_____

_____

_____

_____

_____

_____

_____

_____

_____

_____

_____

_____

_____

_____

Let's jump back to the "Seven Sources of Anxiety" from Chapter Five. We'll find that most of the list are things we can do absloutely nothing about. All except one. Do you have an idea which that one is?

1. Comparisons
2. Preparation
3. Talent
4. Time
5. Small Talk
6. "I don't know what they want."
7. "They're something—I'm nothing."

If you said preparation, you are correct. That's the one we can invest some useful energy into.

Comparing ourselves to others is always a losing battle. Unfortunately, many actors either want to imitate the actors who are successful or they are encouraged to imitate because, sometimes, it seems to work.

When it comes to *talent*, well, talent is mysterious and unexplainable. The most important thing to know about it is that if we work our behinds off, we will nurture the talent we have—if we don't, we won't. And that's really about as much consideration we need give it.

Time and small talk are clearly two things that can only trouble us when our attention is on ourselves, when we are watching ourselves. But that goes against everything acting is about. Sadly, some of the most popular approaches to training actors make the actor even more self-centered and self-conscious; the actor losing all contact with the world of possibilities around him or her. Also, as these thoughts come up in performance, they are fine indications that the actor is not connected to either what he is doing or why he is doing it, he is only connected to "how it is going."

Trying to figure out *what they want* is probably the most futile pursuit of all because not only will they not be able to tell you, they don't know either. Do you hear that? They don't know what they are looking for until you give it to them. They may have an idea, an image in their head, a quality in mind—but they really don't know until they see it. There are just so many casting stories about how great acting in auditions has turned directors in a totally different direction than they thought they were going with a part. The great actors and the great artists are so completely and powerfully themselves—they are originals. Then come all the clones. An acting teacher in NY who I recently interviewed for my book *The Actors Guide to Qualified Acting Coaches,* told me about when Marlon Brando first made it big and how every actor in NY was suddenly wearing Levi's and ripped T-shirts! Isn't this very much like Hollywood or network TV? There is the rare original and then the next thirty movies made to fit into what becomes the latest moneymaking formula.

Can there be any truth to the thought that *they are something and we are nothing*? We must remember that as actors, when we are really doing the work, we make a powerful and vital difference on this planet of ours. It may be reaching just one person who is in your audience tonight. Just one person who needs desperately to witness your struggle as this character, to behold the depth of truth you are courageous enough to share with your fellow actors and with the audience. And from this performance tonight, you have been a catalyst for change in their life or for the taking of action, you may have been a healer of a wounded relationship or a strong reminder of what is of true value. You may never know the impact you've had or you may get a little card saying "Thanks for changing my life!" And in contributing to this one person's world, you have changed the entire world; you have made a difference more far-reaching than you or I could ever imagine. In Arthur Miller's magnificent book *Timebends, A Life*, he shares one of my favorite stories. After the final curtain of the first performance of his play *Death of a Salesman* in Philadelphia, Bernard Gimbel, the head of a large department store chain, was walking up the aisle talking excitedly to his assistant; on that night at the theatre, he gave the order that from that time on, no one in his stores would ever be fired for being overage.

Knowing how important we are, helps us put less energy into trying to make them like us and we become less desperate about the whole thing. (When you date, no matter how hard you try, can you ever really make the girl or the guy fall in love with you?) Remember, you may be burning to get this part, spend weeks in a deep depression because you didn't get it, and then the play doesn't even get produced. Or it does get produced and is so bad it closes in two days. Or you are auditioning for acting schools and you get turned down by your first two choices and you are devastated to end up going to your third choice school. But at your third choice school, you meet and fall in love with the woman you marry, have three children with and spend the rest of your life with. LIFE is surprising, amazing and it won't be controlled!

So, we have examined a lot of the kinds of thoughts that can rule our experience of auditioning. Now, is it possible to just say, "Stop, You Damn Thoughts!" and that's the end of it? I don't think so. You know, if you stop and listen, you can hear that committee of voices in your head talking to you all the time. You know: ordering you around, criticizing you and others, asking why you haven't done this or that with your life, why you are not a success by now, telling you how bad you are for not calling your mother in two weeks and then scolding her for not feeding you better when you were five, demanding you to tell off your lousy boss, warning you not to tell off your lousy boss, etc…From my experience, those voices never really go away, but they do start to fade into the background when we first, accept that we have these thoughts, and next, become deeply involved in what we are doing. If we in any way try to block out or wipe out all these mental "sources of anxiety" we just give them more power. I have found that the mind doesn't respond too well to attack, it does respond well to being embraced as it is. And doesn't that make simple sense? Don't we all respond more favorably when we are embraced for who we are rather than attacked for not being something else? So it is more healthy to simply notice that the thoughts are there with the attitude of, "Wow, that's really interesting," and then get busy with our work.

So, we want the job and we have to want it. Ultimately, it's a matter of inner balance. There has to be a healthy detachment from the results so that we start to live with the attitude that if one door closes, ten others will open up. In this more relaxed fashion, we again return to the work at hand.

And what is the work at hand? As we said before, it's our preparation. Now when I talk about preparation, I'm not just talking about working on the monologue. (Which we have explored in Section One.) I am also talking about your training as an actor—which includes working on the craft of acting, voice and diction, movement and however you go about working on yourself as a human being; your work on the specific audition material you will perform; how you spend your time on the day of your audition; getting relaxed and physically warmed up, as well as emotionally open and available. When we are actively involved in all of these things, the things we truly have control over, we are now in the driver's seat of our audition experience. We may now begin to enjoy a very personal approach to auditioning as an imaginative endeavor, one which excites our creative juices and in which we don't measure our success by the results of the process. The process, which includes the actual audition, becomes fulfilling in itself and if we should get the job, that's the delicious icing on the cake! In this way, when we are turned on by the bigger picture that we have created around the audition event, we are successful before we even walk in the audition door.

chapter 7

The Fundamental Elements
of the Powerful Audition

We've got to have an effective monologue to do at the audition. Which means we must be fully prepared to do it. Right now, in our pursuit of the powerful audition, I want to explore with you some of the fundamental ingredients we have to get into the mix as we continue to develop our audition recipe:

1. Living in the Present

Theatre is an art of presence. I'm not talking about one's demeanor, disposition or sense of savoir faire. I am talking about vitality, truth and aliveness. By whatever means, the actor must re-learn the skill of being in the "right now." (I say "re-learn" because it is not an ability foriegn to us, we were born as masters of this essential capability.) For, as in life, "right now" is the only place where aliveness is available—as opposed to the illusion of the past and the future that most of us live in, most of the time. What do I mean? Well rather than talk about it, let's do a little experiment.

I want you to go and do a house chore. If there are dishes to be washed, wash all the dishes. If the floors need to be washed, do that. Take some time to do a house chore that really needs to be done and as you work, try to give what you are doing your complete attention. Also, **notice where your mind goes as you do the work.** *Do that now, then respond to the statement below.*

○ ○ ○

Take some time to write about what it was like trying to give the chore your complete attention and where you found your mind going when you did the work.

_____

_____

_____

_____

_____

_____

_____

_____

_____

_____

_____

_____

_____

_____

_____

Now I want to do one more experiment. The next time you are in a conversation, a conversation in person with someone, I want you to simply notice where your thoughts are. **Are you giving this person your complete attention or does your mind wander to other concerns?** *Do not read on until you have had a chance to do this.*

○   ○   ○

Take some time to write what you discovered as you brought to awareness the quality of your listening to the other person. Did you really listen? Were you "in & out" in your listening—sometimes really ly with the other person and sometimes lost in some other thoughts? What was it like to start to notice?

_____

_____

_____

_____

_____

_____

_____

_____

_____

_____

_____

_____

_____

_____

A basic truth in life is that it is impossible to do more than one thing at a time fully. We are often doing a number of things at a time and giving none of them our full attention. Think about the impact on our lives. We are eating our oatmeal while we are writing out the checks to pay the overdue bills while we are thinking about what we are going to buy at the electronics store this afternoon—and doing all of it while we are talking on the telephone!—talking on the phone with our friend Sally, who's thinking about what she should wear to an important presentation at work today while she's spreading the peanut butter for her daughter's school lunch and using her big toe to tickle the baby who's on a blanket on the floor starting to cry!

You know, if we are thinking about the electronic store while eating the oatmeal, we'll probably be thinking about the problem with our car's transmission while we are talking with the TV salesman, and when we are on our back, working underneath the car, we'll be thinking about how we should have bought the TV after all and when we get into the shower, we'll be planning what we're going to have for breakfast tomorrow.

How can we really have a relationship with anyone if we are never actually with them, never genuinely available to them? How can we really appreciate or enjoy anything we are doing if we are not giving it our full attention as we are doing it? (How can you enjoy the foreplay if all you're thinking about is the orgasm?) The end result is that we have not really lived a moment of life. Do you get that? We do not get to live a moment of our lives. It's horrifying and very sad!

So, sometimes not being present is missed opportunity after missed opportunity after missed opportunity. Sometimes it is dangerous. Have you ever had the experience of driving a car, trying to tune in a radio station, getting lost in thought and lifting your head up to realize that you don't remember driving the past two miles? "How did I get from there to here? How did I escape from crashing into someone?" Have you ever injured yourself in any way because you just weren't paying attention? Did you ever cut yourself shaving or peel your finger instead of the potato because you were busy thinking about getting revenge on your creepy boss or some such thought?

The fact that the past is over and dead and that the future does not really exist, except as a thought in our head, is certainly not a new concept. It is one of the cornerstones of many ancient philosophies. When we are totally involved with and open to what it is that we are doing, life becomes totally surprising and miraculous. How does this relate to our acting? Acting is doing. I want to say that again—acting is doing. Acting is not "thinking about" or "talking about," it is doing something and doing it fully. Doing at 100%, which means being completely and authentically present to everyone and everything around us. Only in this way can we be truly creative; only in this way can we discover our performance rather than performing what we've already planned out. And as opposed to the majority of acting I see on stage, acting is not pretending to do something, or "making it look like," the basis of all great acting is "really doing something."

2. Really Doing

My great teacher, Sandy Meisner, told us that the foundation of all acting is "the reality of doing." He and my other wonderful acting teacher at the Neighborhood Playhouse, Phil Gushee, taught me this lesson in the most profound ways. (I go into this and other fundamental acting skills in great detail in my series of books, *The Sanford Meisner Approach: An Actor's Workbook*, also published by Smith & Kraus.) Here's a wonderful story which speaks to what "really doing" on stage is all about. A student of Sandy's came to him and said, "Sandy, I'm in a play and I'm having great difficulty with this one moment. It's the moment when I have to ask the girl to marry me. The director wants me to break down and cry when I ask her." Sandy's response was, *"If you want to handle that acting problem, when you ask the girl to marry you—really ask her to marry you."*

Sandy's very simple answer makes it all so clear. When you really do something on stage who gets to be present? You Do! Who is demanded to be present each time you perform? You Are! And really doing forces you to grapple with why the hell you are doing what you are doing in each moment; it forces you to get down to what is personal, authentic and deeply meaningful. Oh Shit, come on now! Every actor in every college acting class across the entire country learns how to name an action and how to play an action—BUT WHY! WHY THE HELL ARE YOU DOING THAT "ACTION?" WHY THE HELL DO YOU NEED TO HAVE THAT RIGHT NOW! WHAT'S MAKING YOU SPEAK THOSE WORDS! AND I MEAN **YOU THE ACTOR**, NOT SOME INTERESTING NOTION YOU HAVE OF SOME IDEA OF SOME "CHARACTER!" Excuse my yelling, it's not directed at you, I just find it so sad and frustrating that so many young actors are coming out of four years of college acting training programs as nothing more than very slick and intellectual fakers. The truth is, to work for real, there's a personal cost involved. Unfortunately, not everyone is taught what paying the price as an actor means, and of those who are, not everyone is interested in or willing to pay the price.

I want to talk with you about one other important lesson in Sandy's response to the actor's difficulty. Again, Sandy said, *"If you want to handle that acting problem, when you ask the girl to marry you—really ask her to marry you."* Notice that he did not say, *"If you want to handle that acting problem, when you ask the girl to marry you—look at her but instead of seeing the actress, see your puppy who you loved and who died when you were five years old."* You see, the actor's challenge was in fulfilling the director's desire to have him cry at this crucial moment in the play. And in Sandy's coaching, he said nothing that would put the actor's attention on emotion or being emotional, he put the actor's attention on the one thing he has real control over—WHAT HE IS DOING! You know, in our lives, we don't really try to be emotional. Only bad actors do. I guarantee you that if I was trying to pull my sister out of a burning car, I would have absolutely no attention on my emotions or whether I was being emotional enough. I'D GET MY SISTER OUT OF THAT CAR!

Here, I'll give you another example. Imagine you are late for a very important meeting, one that is crucial for you to be at. You are very late and you are driving on the highway. It is rush hour and it is raining. Suddenly, you hear a "pop" and the car starts to pull to the left. It's a frightening moment. You quickly put your signal light on and you are able to make it through the stop-and-go traffic over to the right side of the highway and you see an open patch of grass. You pull the car into the clearing and come to a stop. Then it comes back to you—the meeting! You look at your watch and realize that the meeting will begin in twenty minutes. You jump out of the car, into the rain and you quickly start to take off the flat tire. Now as you are changing the tire, do you think that you will be thinking, *"This is the biggest opportunity in my life and I'm late. God, I have to get emotional right now. I have to make myself cry and throw a fit and be really upset."* Pretty silly, right? Probably, you'll be putting all of your attention and efforts into getting the tire changed. Now, as you do it, you may get pissed off and kick the car. You may be scared and deeply sad about losing this big chance. You may cry, scream and bang your head on the ground. You may even try not to get emotional because it is making getting the tire changed more difficult. But I guarantee you, there is not a second that you think about getting yourself into some emotional state or criticize yourself for not being emotional enough. **Your emotions come to life freely and on their own as your attention is on what you are doing.** Of course, the greater the meaning in what you are doing, the more alive you become emotionally. This is true in our lives and it is true in our acting.

Your true engagement with what you are doing, especially with very specific and personal meaning, brings life to the stage because it brings YOU TO LIFE. "Really doing" has an impact on your partners on stage, on you and on the audience—an impact which is unavoidable, compelling and out of your control. It is this aspect of acting that makes your performance unique to you because **when you are really doing what you are doing, only you—in the whole world—are able to do it in just that way.** You want to be an original? Begin to really do what you are doing.

I want to move into another exercise now:

For one day, from the time you get up until the time you go to bed, you will try to make everyone you come in contact with comfortable to be with you. Wherever you are, you will try to make whoever you are with feel at home with you. Do not explain that this is what you are doing and do not tell anyone how you want them to feel. (So you would not say, "I want you to feel comfortable.") Using all of yourself, **while you are talking and while you are listening,** *make continued attempts to have everyone you are with feel comfortable to be with you. Do this by* **how you are being** *with them.*

At the end of this day, just before going to bed, do the writing exercise on the following page.

On this page and the following blank page, write about your experience of today's experiment. What was it like to make the attempt during the course of your day? Talk about some of the ways you found to be effective in accomplishing your goal. How was it different with different people? How did people respond to what you were doing? What did trying to make others be at home with you, **do to you**—*how did it make you feel inside? Did you feel awkward or artificial? Did it become easier and more natural the more you did it? As you were involved in this "doing," what did you notice about your own attention and interest? Talk about anything else you discovered.*

_____

_____

_____

_____

_____

_____

_____

_____

_____

_____

_____

_____

_____

_____

_____

_____

3. Embracing What's Happening

Simply, this means accepting exactly what is happening as it's happening. We can look at this in a literal sense. Here's an example: You drive to work everyday. For the last month you stayed in the left lane of the highway and, until you had to get onto the exit ramp, you were able to drive at sixty miles per hour without slowing down a single time. Today, once again, you are in the left lane driving at sixty miles per hour but—how can this be?— you see lots of red lights up ahead. As you get closer, you see cars slowing down in all of the lanes. But you have driven at sixty everyday and that's how you like it, that's what has become comfortable and that's how you want it to stay. So, you're gonna drive at sixty today no matter what the other cars appear to be doing!

Ridiculous, right? But that's a bad habit many of us have in life. In so many ways, we avoid dealing with what is happening. We pretend not to see what is happening so that we can stay in the comfort zone of what happened before, what we want to be happening and what we think should happen.

Of course, the same tendency carries over to our acting. How? Let's say you are in a play. In the first read-through, you get positive responses from the director and the other cast members to what you're doing. They laugh and seem to enjoy your performance. So then, you do your best to repeat what you did in the first read-through in the rehearsals. As the responses decrease from the others, you try harder to do what you did in that first read-through. Then, on opening night, the audience gives you some of the laughs you got at the first read-through. On night two, three and four, they don't laugh as much, so you try harder to do what you did on opening night. Do you think there is any space for any real acting to occur in this kind of process?

There is another more subtle and elusive aspect of this which demands that us actors be wide open, available and agile in every possible way. You know, when actors are doing the real work, no two nights of a play are ever going to be quite the same. Why? Because when you are alive and in the moment, YOU are never the same and neither are your acting partners. In this way, the play becomes a wonderful improvisation. This does not mean that the work the actors and the director have done goes out the window. No. The richly layered texture of meanings that you have uncovered in the rehearsals remain, the spine and the throughline of the play and for each actor holds true, all the moments you worked, the actions and personalizations, all the blocking, certainly every single one of the playwright's words— all the specific and meticulous elements worked out in rehearsals must be there. And all of it, all of that work, becomes the catapult launching you into a fabulous rollercoaster ride with your partners on stage; each of you enjoying the discovery of each moment as it occurs "right now"; as each moment is created for the first time in precisely this way. So, when you are present in each moment, and as you freely **embrace exactly what is happening** and allow it to take you to what's next—well now, you see, the play truly is an improvisation because you really don't know what's going to happen next. Now, the audience gets their moneys worth. They are not seeing last night's performance, they are seeing living human beings in the act of creation right in front of their eyes. The audience feels like they are peeking through a window and witnessing something very private. And that is exactly what we want!

Of course, there are some inner hurdles to get past if we are to accomplish what we've been discussing. Now, when these issues come up for you off-stage, that's one thing to take a look at. What I want to talk about here is when these thoughts plague you **AS YOU ARE ACTING**. Some of these internal obstacles are:

1. Resting on the security blanket of what has happened in any previous performance.

2. Holding on to how you think you should be in every moment.

3. Trying to control how every moment should go.

4. Stopping to think about or decide how you should handle what is happening.

5. Judging, criticizing or evaluating yourself or your partner when a moment does not meet up to your expectations -OR- patting yourself on the back and congratulating yourself when you think you were just marvelous in any moment.

The first four just mentioned must lead to a predominant way of dealing with the guaranteed newness of how things will actually be happening every time you perform. Do you have an idea of what that way would be? Write down your thoughts here:

_____

_____

_____

_____

_____

_____

_____

_____

In this restricted approach, you must **deny** anything new. This denial creates an inner battle and out of that battle, a wave of tension that paralyzes your acting instrument. And "what is happening" is coming at you so quickly on stage—which is why we must continually hone our ability to "go with" what is happening rather than to fight against it in any way. Remember, we are talking about live theatre here. So, not only are all the subtle qualities of everything going on in your acting partners new each night, surprising and unforseen things are going to happen on stage:

• The other actor forgets to say a line which needs to be said so that you can say your line.
• The arm of the couch you are leaning on breaks and falls to the floor.
• There's no wine to pour into the glasses to make the toast.
• The roof starts to leak right over you and the actress in the middle of your love scene.
• You open the door to make your exit and the door comes right off the hinges, etc…

Most actors are horrified by these unexpected incidents; they freeze and try to make believe it's not happening. (Which immediately communicates to the audience as a lie.) But the only time these events become disasters is when the actor considers them disasters rather than welcoming them as fun new things to work with. When we are free enough to immediately "go with it," we are able to discover uncanny ways of dealing with everything. These "mistakes," handled in this manner, are gifts that often turn into the most beautiful and breathtaking moments of life on stage.

You know, athletes speak of these same issues when they talk about being effective in their sports. I use basketball a lot as an example because I have played in competitive pickup games for years and, I love basketball! You and your team have the simple and specific goal to get the ball in the net more often than the other team does. And you pursue that goal along with your teammates in every possible way. At the same time you are demanded to give up any control as to how the game should go and, you must be continually and fully available to accept and capitalize on the opprtunities the game dishes up to you. Also, every game presents a thousand unexpected moments where you must respond without the luxury or the time to stop and consider how to do it. As in acting, the very moment you stop to think about how you should respond, "Should I pass or should I shoot?" **you're out of the ball game!**

I want to repeat point number five from above: *Judging, criticizing or evaluating yourself or your partner when a moment does not meet up to your expectations. -OR- Patting yourself on the back and congratulating yourself when you think you were just marvelous in any moment.* You see, theatre is an art where the actor must not stop to corroborate what he or she has just created. But in the midst of acting the scene in the play (or the monologue at the audition) how easy it is to get lost in thoughts like: "God I just screwed that up!" or, "Boy this audience is quiet, what's going wrong here?" or, "Damn him! I hate when he delivers that line with that stupid smile on his face!" or, "Man I'm good, I'm really good! I hope that reviewer is here tonight!" And once these thoughts set in, you isolate yourself in your head while the play goes whisking right by you. YOU are no longer really there. You go into a kind of "autopilot" mode, your mouth saying words while your brain is busy with other matters. When you walk off stage, if your working with an actor who is **awake**, you'll get comments like, "Where the hell were you tonight?" or, "I don't appreciate being left alone out there pal!"

I'll tell you, fresh out of studying at the Neighborhood Playhouse, I got a lead in an Off-Broadway play and I worked opposite an actor who was much too busy embracing himself to be available to anything going on around him. It's very upsetting and very lonely being on a stage with people who aren't present. Avoid, in any way you can, working with actors who are more interested in themselves than in the characters they play. Certainly, work like crazy not to be that kind of actor yourself!

4. Being Relaxed

When we begin to put our attention on what we have control over, when we are fully prepared with our audition piece and when the first three building blocks we have been talking about are functioning—*living in the present, really doing and embracing what's happening*—we discover a new and wonderful sense of relaxation in our work. I'm not talking about being relaxed on just a physical level, which is also essential; I'm talking about a very deep state of ease, a freedom from worry and constraint, a kind of liberation of the spirit which mobilizes within us a vitality and a readiness to take action.

chapter 8

Now What?

You know, I have talked your ears off and this would be a good time for me to wrap things up. There are lots of audition books that discuss the actual audition itself in terms of logistics and what to expect from signing in to introducing yourself, etc. So, I'm not going to address that except to say what I think is the most important thing to realize: nothing matters to the people watching you as much as one thing—THE WORK YOU DO. It's not about your clothes, the way your hair came out today or if you are a perfect person. They want to see great work. And if anyone you are auditioning for is more interested in your hair, why would you want to work with them anyway?

The point of this book was to begin to free you up so that you can put your attention on what is important. When you do and when you are fully prepared, you might just begin to actually enjoy your auditions. The people watching you want to see that you can realize the demands of the material you chose to share with them and that you LOVE TO DO IT! As any audience, they want to be moved, shaken, surprised, and lifted out of the canned dental office music that is lurking all around us—trying to suck up our lives.

Clearly, this book doesn't offer everything you need. You can only get all that you need by your continual pursuit of growing in your own, individual craft of acting and learning more about yourself as a human being on a troubled planet. Study and look around you, study and look around you. Be a continual student—wherever you are, in class and out. It's not an eight-week deal and it's not a two-year deal. It's a lifelong process. And if my little book contributes at all to that process being a more fulfilling and enjoyable one, then I'm a smashing success.

Well, it has been quite an amazing journey for me in sharing with you in this book and I hope that the experiences you've had in "doing" the book have been valuable for you. Please feel free to write or call me with any questions about the book or the exercises in it—I'd love to hear from you. You will find my address and telephone number on my Bio page. If you want to get more into the kind of work we have done together, you might enjoy one of my other books, *The Sanford Meisner Approach: An Actor's Workbook* and my three sequels to that book.

Thank you for your time and attention. I wish you all the success in the world and a life rich in health and joy.

Be well my friend!

Love, Larry